TEA
of
HIMACHAL PRADESH

TEA
of
HIMACHAL PRADESH

Ram Gopal Sud

Published for Institute of Integrated Himalayan Studies,
(UGC Centre of Excellence), H.P. University, Shimla

SHIPRA

ISBN: 81-7541-349-2

First Published in India in 2007

Tea of Himachal Pradesh

Published by:
SHIPRA PUBLICATIONS
115-A, Vikas Marg, Shakarpur
Delhi-110092, INDIA
Phone: 91-11-65277210, 91-11-22500954
Fax: 91-11-22458662
E-mail: info@shiprapublications.com
www.shiprapublications.com

Foreword

Himachal Pradesh is a rich state in terms of its natural resources. With rich diversity, the state holds great future on the path to emerging as one of the prosperous states of the country. The diversity in terms of climate, altitude and soil provide potential for the development of varied agro-systems. In the Hindu Kush Himalayan range, agro-forestry systems are accepted as one of the good practices for the development of people living in the mountains.

The cultivation of tea particularly in Kangra district of Himachal Pradesh needs special attention. Kangra tea is well known for its distinctiveness. In the past, India has been largest producer and exporter of tea. Tea drinking certainly became established in China many centuries before it had even been heard of in the West. Lu Yu wrote the first definitive book on tea, the *Ch'a Ching* or Tea Classic in 800 AD. However, tea is often thought of as being a quintessentially British drink for over 350 years. The cultivation and treatment of tea could not flourish in Himachal Pradesh due to various reasons. Deliberate and planned measures fell short not only in motivating the tea producers but also in evolving strategies for marketing and developing taste for Kangra Tea. The quality of Kangra tea is considered to be comparatively quite high. A handful researchers have worked on various aspects pertaining to the cultivation and marketing of Kangra tea. It is by and large accepted that this industry should be promoted. It has the potential to emerge as a good source of employment and income generation.

Realizing the importance of this resource, Institute of Integrated Himalayan Studies (UGC Centre of Excellence), Himachal Pradesh University, Shimla, after consultation with various experts decided to study the status of tea industry. Dr. Ram Gopal Sud, a renowned scientist working in Agriculture University, Palampur agreed to take up this task of consolidating information regarding agro-techniques, agronomy, plant protection, nursery raising practices in vogue and ongoing research work on various aspects of tea. The work done by Dr. Sud is based on his wide research experience and first hand information. I am hopeful that this volume "Tea of Himachal Pradesh" would provide exhaustive understanding about the present status of Kangra Tea. It will provide plenty of data and insight for formulating new strategies for further development of tea industry in Himachal Pradesh. Dr. Ram Gopal Sud deserves appreciation for this meticulous work.

1.1.2007

Prof. Yoginder Verma
Director
Institute of Integrated Himalayan Studies
(UGC Centre of Excellence)
Himachal Pradesh University, Shimla–171 005

Acknowledgements

World tea scenario that we perceive today is attributed to the numerous peoples' vision, innovation and yeoman service by a large number of people. Any book is always possible by consolidating these efforts and this one is no exception. My sincere thanks are due to those people who have toiled to develop tea cultivation and processing against all odds to make the "cup that cheers" and led to many a songs praising our most delightful brew.

My sincere thanks are also due to late Lala Kunj Bihari Lal Butail and Lala Brij Bihari Lal Butail of Bundla Tea Estate, Mr. Krishan Gopal Butail and Shri Pyare Lal Butail of Sungal Tea Estate, Thakur Balwant Singh of Mansimbal Tea Estate, Mrs. Chander Prabha Kamal Jeet, Mr. Naveen Sareen of Chandpur Tea Estate, Mr. Neelam Sood of Sidhbari Tea Estate and Shri Ghanshyam jee (Lambardar) who lent me time and patient hearing to satiate my inquisitiveness and transformed my ignorance into knowledge.

My sincere thanks are also due to Dr. Parmvir Singh Ahuja, Director, Institute of Himalayan Bioresource Technology (IHBT), Dr. Satish Chander Sharma, Director of Research, CSKHP Krishi Vishvavidyalaya (CSKHPKV), Mr. Prahlad Chettri, Development Officer, Regional Office, Tea Board India and Mr. B.S. Chauhan, Assistant Director (Tea) for providing relevant information on Tea of Himachal Pradesh.

Thanks are also due to Dr. Anil Sood, Head, Biotechnology Division, IHBT, Dr. S.K. Sugha, Head, Department of Plant Pathology and Dr. Satish Paul, Scientist (Tea Breeder), Department of Tea Husbandry and Technology, CSKHPKV, Palampur for providing useful inputs. Special thanks are also due to Mr. Radhesh Chander Sharma; my Mathematician friend who captured rare documents, reproduced herein, in his camera.

The financial support from the Director, Institute of Integrated Himalayan Studies, HP University, Shimla is thankfully acknowledged.

It is inevitable in a topic which is enormous and complex that there will be occasional errors; those are mine.

Ram Gopal Sud

Prologue

Tea was introduced in the 'pulum' region of Himachal Pradesh by Dr. Jameson, the Superintendent of the Botanical North-West Provinces in 1849. The establishment of tea industry dates back to 1860s when the first tea plantation established by the Government at Holta was bought by Major Stutt in 1866. Nurtured by numerous English and native growers, the Kangra valley tea became famous and the industry emerged as a major employment resource in the region. Tea also witnessed repercussions of 1905 earthquake, First World War and inexperienced managements. Lack of technical guidance, shortage of labour, low yield, low returns and reinvestments, neglect and abandonment of tea plantation etc. led the tea industry of Himachal Pradesh into a hapless state.

Tea has been surviving due to the Government initiatives and growers' enterprise. Tea Board India, Government of Himachal Pradesh, Institute of Himalayan Bioresource Technology (IHBT) and CSK Himachal Pradesh Krishi Vishvavidyalaya (CSKHPKV) also rally-rounded the tea of Himachal Pradesh. Development of agro-techniques for tea cultivation, standardization of doses and schedules of fertilizers, plant protection, improvement in tea quality, breeding of new tea varieties and raising nurseries, micropropagation of tea plants, establishment of tea processing units, rejuvenation of neglected and abandoned tea gardens, organizing management training programmes, etc. have been the major foci of research, development and extension activities. Four Cooperative Tea Factories one in district Mandi at Bir and three in district Kangra at Palampur, Sidhbari and Baijnath were established with a view to provide firm footing to the Kangra tea. Tea Board India also provided financial assistance for rehabilitation and modernization of private and cooperative factories.

Because of the cumulative efforts of the agencies involved in the welfare of the tea industry following achievements are noteworthy:

- Agro-techniques in tea cultivation were standardized to enhance the productivity.
- Disease and pest control measures were tailored to suit the regional needs.
- Nutritional status of soils under tea gardens and green tea shoots was assessed.
- Two new tea clones Kangra Asha (KVK-1) and Kangra Jwala (KVK-3) (with uniform and vigorous growth, resistant to draught, hail and frost and high valuation) were released.
- Tea nurseries were established to provide subsidized young tea plants.
- Data on quality aspects was provided to cooperative tea factory.
- Rejuvenation of abandoned and neglected area was undertaken.
- Financial assistance in the form of soft loans and subsidies in fertilizers, farm and irrigation equipments and for rejuvenation was provided.
- Financial assistance was also provided to cooperative and private tea processing units for the modernization of machinery to improve the quality and valuation of Kangra tea.

The Palampur Cooperative Tea Factory Limited, Palampur won Chairman's Challenge Trophy for quality tea production and also for highest all-India price amongst the cooperative factories in 1991.

Most of the recommendations of the 1997 Expert Committee Report were implemented and did show positive results. The production of tea increased in spite of the fact that the area under tea in Himachal Pradesh has dwindled. However, the average yield of tea in Himachal Pradesh is no where near the national average.

Efforts are afoot to bring new area under tea cultivation. However, it has become imperative to conduct a fresh survey by an expert committee to ascertain the present status of tea in the region. New strategies particularly aimed at enhancing yield, improving quality, reduction in cost of production, inter-cropping, organic farming, product diversification and enhancing the demand for Kangra valley tea are required to be formulated.

The major thrust areas of endeavours include:

- Rejuvenation and repair of soil in the tea gardens.

- Development of new clones that would yield several times the current yield.
- Development of genetically engineered plants having short dormancy period and adaptable to changing weather conditions.
- Acquiring ISO ratings for tea gardens and factories of Himachal Pradesh.
- Creating awareness among tea growers about the use of organic manure and biological control of pests.
- Decreasing cost of production to increase profits and reinvestments.
- Validating the distinct qualities of Kangra tea.
- Evaluating the antioxidant property due to polyphenols in tea.
- Using established health benefits of tea in promotional campaigns.
- Conducting opinion poll surveys to assess consumers' predilection.
- Focusing research on product innovation and diversification.
- Using appellations of origin under its own brand name and logo specifying the qualities attributable to the Kangra tea in promotional campaigns.
- Using modern communication means for advertisement and marketing.
- Last but not the least using modern management skills to develop human resource.

The studies reported herein emphasize the accomplishments of various research and development organizations. This one report will help to identify the shortcomings and steps needed to overcome them. It is earnestly anticipated that it would help open new avenues to promote Kangra tea. It is envisaged that the present studies offering an insight into the present status of tea if coupled with an extensive survey will also serve as guiding tool in formulating new strategies for the development of tea industry of Himachal Pradesh to boost the economy of the state.

Contents

Foreword 5

Acknowledgements 7

Prologue 8

1. Historical Background 13

2. Research and Development: Agrotechnique Management and Extension 29

3. Research and Development: Nutrients, Quality and Breeding 61

4. Research Gaps 98

5. Identification of Areas of Short-term and Long-term Research 101

6. Policy Implications 103

7. Action Plan 119

Selected Bibliography 122

Index 127

1

Historical Background

The first drink discovered by Adam after water was tea............

"The history of tea in India is a glorious record of continuous development of one of our foremost industries and a valuable national asset", Sanjiva Reddy.

The establishment of Indian Tea Industry is undoubtedly one of the most important developments during the nineteenth century. In 1833 when the treaty with China, under which tea was imported expired; there was great concern among tea traders. There was something about the tea — a tradition, a charm, romance, which was shared from the highest to the lowest. How could England rule the waves without a nice cup of tea? The tea industry in India was established, primarily to meet the demand of the Imperial power which was already the World's largest importer and consumer of tea. Tea drinking habit developed on slowly among Indians. Of a total crop of 270 million kilos domestic consumption was only 70 million kilos by 1947. However, with increasing prosperity, availability and population growth, tea today has become country's favourite beverage. India emerged not only as the World's largest producer of tea but, also as its biggest consumer by the end of twentieth century.

Some historians believe that tea has been drunk in India in one form or another from prehistoric times. However, tea plants which had been growing wild in Assam were collected; first by Robert Bruce (1823) and later on by his younger brother, Charles Alexander Bruce, which were declared not to be the genuine tea. However, in 1834 when the British Government decided to initiate tea cultivation in India, Lord Cavendish Bentinck, the Governor General of Bengal set up the historic Tea Committee to identify the areas for cultivating tea on a commercial scale. The indigenous tea plants were now declared to be genuine tea 'not different from the plant of China'. What followed next; was that the province that were once jungle and swamp were transformed by British capital and enterprise into a land of neat tea-gardens with almost all the modern amenities.

Enterprising Englishmen succeeded in learning the guarded art of tea cultivation and manufacture from Chinese and escaped to bring back the knowledge. Tea industry had to pass through years of experimentation at number of research stations and in laboratories where every process in the cultivation, growth and manufacture of tea was developed gradually. Through each failure, however, the technology was perfected. Finally, after years of trial and error, fortunes made and lost; the English tea plantations in India and other parts of Asia flourished.

Guided by the fact that in the mountainous tracts of Northern and Eastern frontiers several species of plants were found indigenous which were also natives of China, Dr. Royle, Superintendent of Botanical Gardens, Saharanpur recommended the cultivation of tea in the Himalayas. In order to give a fair trial to tea cultivation, Lord Bentinck, distributed plants raised from imported China seeds in the sub-Himalayan region. Dr. Falconer, Superintendent of Botanical Gardens succeeded in growing tea plants in Saharanpur in 1838. From the Kumaon Hills a small quantity of China hybrid seeds and plants along with seeds obtained from China were transported to be planted in Kangra district of erstwhile Punjab. "Nassan Tea Company" was the first that came into existence.

Dr. Jameson, the Superintendent of the Botanical North-West Provinces, travelled through Kangra valley to ascertain feasibility to grow tea in the region. He not only recommended tea cultivation in the lower slopes of Dhauladhar range of Himalayas but, after four months returned with young tea plants obtained from the nurseries at Almora and Dehra Dun in 1849. Three spots, one at Kangra, another at Nagrota Bagwan and the third at Bhawarna were selected for experimenting on propagating young tea plants. The experiments succeeded at Nagrota Bagwan and Bhawarna; however, the plants did not survive at Kangra. This led to the establishment of tea plantation by the Government at Holta in the year 1852 under the auspices of "Hailey Nagar Tea Estate". This plantation was ultimately sold to Major Stutt in 1866.

The success of Government plantation led to the beginning of private enterprises. British officers namely Major Paske — through negotiations with zamindars for transfer of waste lands and Mr. Eqerton, Deputy Commissioner, Kangra — by relaxing the forest rules; further facilitated the availability of land for tea cultivation. By the year 1880, many plantations were developed covering an area of 4180 hectares extending from Jogindernagar (Mandi) to Shahpur (Kangra). Major Paske in his Report of the Year (1872) mentioned the following "...the outturn of tea amounted to 29,312 lbs., the tea realizing by public auction an average of Rs. 1 per lb., ... In 1859 and 1860 the success of the Government plantation led to the introduction of private enterprise and capital, but the operations of European settlers were retarded by the difficulties experienced in obtaining land...". According to Mr. R.A. Ballard, Honorary Secretary, Kangra Tea Planters' Association: there were 34 gardens owned by Europeans of which three were owned by large companies registered under the Limited Liability Act, two were large unregistered companies and the remainder were smaller tea estates each owned by one or more proprietors. Holta Tea Company was the only company whose shares were quoted in the Calcutta Stock Exchange.

"The best sale of Kangra tea during 1892 was an invoice of 152 packages containing 4,058 lbs. of tea from the Kangra Valley Tea Company Limited,..; this same company sold during 1892; 41,848 lbs of tea on the London Market...; it also sold during the same year 34,453 lbs. on the Calcutta market.., and these results were considered very good."

Some 700 acres of new land were brought under cultivation between 1892 and 1905 by European and native proprietors, but similar area of old and unprofitable tea had gone out of cultivation. The devastating earthquake of April 4, 1905 in the valley took its toll on tea industry as well. The majority of the factories were razed to the ground; some tea growing areas were ruined. A large number of planters lost their lives and most of those who survived migrated to Darjeeling and Assam. Although a few small estates continued to grow tea but, the progress in the tea sector halted as there was acute shortage of manpower and tea manufacturing expertise. In the post 1914 years the labour problem was further worsened by the World war as many young men from the valley were lured away by the money to join the armed forces. The net outcome was that even the Kangra valley tea planters and the proprietors who dared to stay back after 1905 earthquake were forced to sell their lands and factories in order to migrate to the tea growing areas of Darjeeling and Assam. The new owners were caught in a vicious cycle. They lacked expertise in tea cultivation and manufacture; factories were in poor condition. Consequently quality of tea deteriorated and prices were unremunerative.

1.1 Some Landmarks

Letter and Minutes of the Founders Meeting

Courtesy: Lala Brij Bihari Lal Butail, Bundla Tea Estate, Palampur, Kangra (H.P.)

Thursday the 27 January, 1898: Formation of Kangra Tea Association

Nassan Palampur

Kangra Valley
12th January 1898

To the Proprietors & Lessees of Kangra Valley Tea Property
Gentlemen,

I think the time has come when the Kangra Valley Tea industry might be more ably represented by Proprietors than it is at present by young and often inexperienced Managers, most of whom are here today & gone tomorrow, and whose personal stake in the industry is confined to their pay & their perquisites.

I propose therefore with your assistance & cooperation to start a representative association to be called "The Kangra Tea Association" to protect & push the interests of the Tea Industry, & more especially to try and revive the Green Tea Trade with Central Asia.

The following are the lines on which I would suggest the formation of a new association:

I. Members must be Proprietor & Lessees to be entitled to vote.
II. Mangers may be admitted (by ballot) if their proprietors signify their wish for it in writing, but shall not be allowed to vote.
III. Nature proprietors of Estates of 20 acres to be invited to form.
IV. Subscriptions to be limited to Rs. 8/- per annum for Estates of over 50 acres and Rs. 4 per annum for Estates of smaller acreage.

V. The formation of subsidiary clubs such as social and medical ....assisted.

If you approve of this scheme......be glad of you with vote your willingness to cooperate at foot hereof — together with or remarks that may suggest themselves to you.

Should a sufficient number of names be entered I will at an early date call a meeting to draft rules & organize the proposed association.

Yours faithfully
Sd.
H. Compton

I am in favour of this and will join with pleasure.	Sd. Culbard Soungul 12/1/98
Do Do	Sd. Andrew Turnbull Palampur 12/1/98
I certainly agree and will write.......	Sd. Turner, Tanda 12/1/98
I agree, and join with pleasure	Sd. W.H. Prachey
Will join	Sd. T.J. Greensill 13/1/98
Will join	Sd.

Founders Meeting

Minutes of the first meeting of the Kangra Tea Association held at Nassan, Palampur at 2 p.m. on Thursday *27 January, 1898*

The notice convening a meeting of Tea Proprietors for the purpose of forming an association was read, and it was *proposed* by W.M. Culbard and *seconded* by W.T.J. Greensill and resolved that we the undersigned Proprietors and Lessees of Tea Property in the Kangra Valley hereby constitute ourselves an association under the name of the *Kangra Tea Association.*

Sd.
H. Compton
Secretary

Sd.
W. Andrew Turnbull
President
W. Culbard
S.D. Turner
T.J. Greensill
W.H. Prachey

April, 1898: Affiliation of the Kangra Tea Association with Indian Tea Association.

1924: Kangra Tea Planters Association was formed.

1930: Name of the association was changed to Kangra Valley Tea Planters' Association.

1930s: Indian Tea Licensing Committee allotted quota for exporting tea. (Quota rights were sold to the other areas).

1938: Proposal from the Cooperative Department to organize tea industry on cooperative basis. (The association did not agree).

1950: Labour Commissioner, Punjab offered interest free loans for the purchase of equipments and machinery from the Government. (Proposal did not materialize).

1953/54: Opening of the office by the Tea Board of India. (The office was initially at Dharamshala that was later on shifted to Palampur).

1962: The Kangra Tea Planters' Supply & Marketing Cooperative Industrial Society Limited formed.

1962: The state Government and the Tea Board of India launched scheme "Improvement of Tea Culture in Hilly areas of North-Western Regions".

1962: Establishment of Tea Experiment station at Palampur. (Now part of Chaudhary Sarwan Kumar Himachal Pradesh Krishi Vishvavidyalaya).

1964: The first cooperative factory was established at Bir (Mandi District).

1978: Creation of Himachal Pradesh Krishi Vishvavidyalaya.

1979: The State government appointed Technical Officer Tea in the Department of Industries. (The TOT's office is in Palampur).

1980: The Palampur Cooperative Tea Factory Limited, Palampur commissioned.

1981: Third cooperative factory was established at Baijnath.

1984: Fourth cooperative tea factory started at Sidhbari.

1984: Establishment of the Council of Scientific and Industrial Research Complex at Palampur.

2005: Geographical Indication status for Kangra tea.

OUTPUT~2.EPS; Plate 1

Memorial Diploma Awarded to Messrs Sterling and Culbard Glasgow International Exhibition 1888

Courtesy: Mr. K.G. Butail and Mr Pyare Lal Butail, Sungal Tea Estate, Kangra (H.P.)

Certificate of Merit of the 3rd Class Awarded to Sterling and Culbard Estate for Tea, International Exhibition Calcutta 1883-84

Courtesy: Mr. K.G. Butail and Mr. Pyare Lal Butail, Sungal Tea Estate, Kangra (H.P.)

Gold Medal Awarded to Bundla Tea Estate at London

Courtesy: Lala Kunj Bihari Lal Butail, Bundla Tea Estate, Kangra (H.P.)

Certificate of Merit Awarded for Tea to Bundla Tea Estate at 44th Indian National Congress, Lahore, Congress Exhibition (1929) and the All-India Exhibition of Arts and Industries Punjab (1937-38)

Courtesy: Lala Kunj Bihari Lal Butail, Bundla Tea Estate, Kangra (H.P.)

1.2 Introduction

Himachal Pradesh, the land of Gods and Goddesses, is located between Latitude 30° 22' 40" N to 33° 12' 20" N, Longitude 75° 45' 55" E to 79° 04' 20" E and altitude ranging between 350 meters to 6,975 meters above mean sea level (amsl). It is blessed with unique geography, complex geological structure and a rich flora. The areas Dalhousie of district Chamba, Jogindernagar of district Mandi and Dharamshala and Palampur of district Kangra comprise its wet sub-temperate zone.

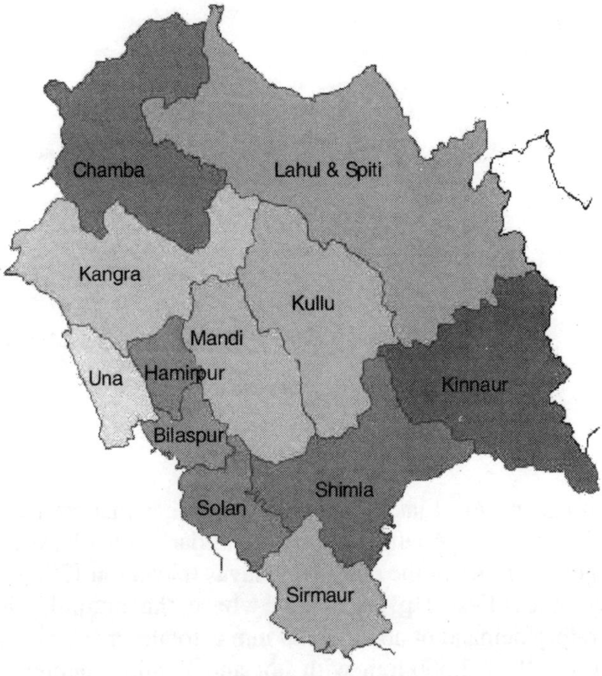

Himachal Pradesh

Palampur (Latitude: 32° 07' 15.68" N, Longitude: 76° 31' 47.26" E altitude: 4275 feet amsl) is a panoramic valley that is situated in the lap of gorgeous Dhauladhar range of mighty Himalayas. Palampur came into prominence when Dr. Jameson, the Superintendent of the Botanical North-West Provinces introduced the tea plant in 1849. The word Palam was derived from "pulum" the local jargon for lots of water. The bush thrived and the town became focus of the European and native tea estate owners. The tea of Himachal Pradesh, popularly known as Kangra Tea or Kangra Valley Tea with its center at Palampur has been acclaimed internationally.

"...He mentioned that he had just opened a sealed bottle of Kangra Valley Tea made over forty years ago, which, though slightly flat, still retained much of its original flavour and body". So exclaimed an elderly and well-known tea buyer in Landon in January, 1954.

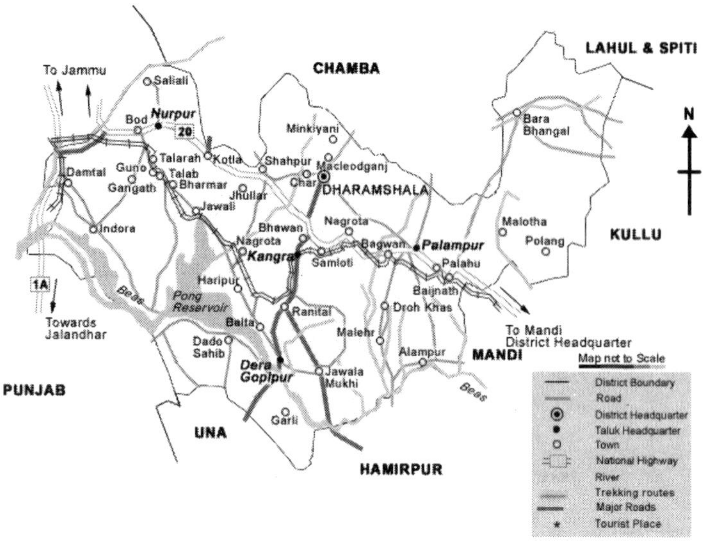

The Kangra local jat, China type tea bushes that are more than 150 years old, have small, erect, hard and dark green leaves, grows on the gentle slopes of the outer Himalayas (elevation 1290 m above mean sea level, soil pH 4.8-5.8) where the annual potential transpiratory demand of about 1,100 mm is totally met by the annual mean rainfall of 2,500 mm with hot and humid summers (mean temperature maximum 36°C, minimum 16.5°C) and cold winters. Because of its weather-related growth-pattern plucking is done from April to October. Owing to low temperatures during the winter months the tea bushes experience complete dormancy for about 120-150 days. In Himachal Pradesh commercial tea is manufactured from the succulent shoots (two to three leaves and a bud) plucked repeatedly from perennial tea [*Camellia sinensis* (L) O Kuntze] plant at appropriate intervals.

Since the opening of the office of Assistant Director, Tea Board at Dharamshala (later on it was shifted to Palampur) during 1953-54, the Tea Board of India has been constantly rendering help to the tea industry of this region through development schemes. In 1962, the State Government and the Tea Board of India jointly launched a scheme "Improvement of Tea Culture in Hilly Areas of North-Western Regions" and the Tea Experimental Station was established at Palampur. At the same time the Tea Board of India recognized the newly founded "The Kangra Tea Planters' Supply and Marketing Cooperative Industrial Society Limited". The aim of the society was to supply inputs to the tea growers and promote the sale of Kangra tea by opening auction house at Amritsar. The Board also provided financial assistance and grant-in-aid for setting up the cooperative tea factories, tea nurseries and demonstration plots, subsidies for reclamation, rejuvenation and other developmental activities.

However, the average yields 273 kg/ha and 132 kg/ha of Kangra tea recorded in 1963 and 1980, respectively were all time low compared to the all India average yields of 1036 kg/ha and 1537 kg/ha during the same period, respectively, was a matter of concern for the State Government. Kangra tea witnessed 300 per cent decline in yield and earned 40 per cent of the average of Calcutta auction price in spite of its inherent quality. The State Agriculture University, Palampur and the Institute of Himalayan Bioresource Technology (IHBT) erstwhile Council of Scientific and Industrial Research (CSIR) Complex, Palampur were involved actively in the development of tea cultivation, tea production and tea processing since their inception in November, 1978 and July, 1983, respectively. The Government of Himachal Pradesh was also keen to develop the State Tea Industry. The Department of Industries, Government of Himachal Pradesh made available finances to erstwhile CSIR Complex, Palampur to gather information on various aspects of Himachal Tea Industry.

A comprehensive survey of the tea planters conducted by CSIR during 1984-85 showed that there were 1660 tea planters cultivating an area of 2063 hectares under tea crop. Of this 80 per cent of growers were sharing about one-fifth of the area, each with less than one hectare holdings and producing about 2,00,000 kg green leaf annually. Six to seven planters (about 0.4 per cent) with a holding size of more than 40 hectares produced 6,50,000 kg of green leaf per year. Eight families were wholly dependent on tea cultivation and production for their livelihood. About 60 per cent of the tea planters did not have income from tea. Tea planters were not much aware about the use of weedicides, insecticides, miticides and fungicides etc. Nutrients except nitrogen were rarely used in tea gardens. The labour employment with an average of 0.37 labour per hectare was extremely low. Shortage of labour, lack of technical guidance and financial assistance and unfenced fields were recognized as the main problems faced by tea growers of Himachal Pradesh. Very low yield followed by less returns and thereby negligible plough-back of income to the industry were held responsible for the neglect of tea growing areas and the hapless state of tea industry in Himachal Pradesh. The Survey Report (1980-83) on Tea Gardens of Himachal Pradesh under Technical Advice categorically mentioned, "Tea business appears to be subsidiary occupation for most of the growers. Perhaps that is why a majority of the tea growers have not bothered to seek any technical advice from different institutions dealing with the tea Research and Development. Secondly, due to lack of proper extension services even the existing institutions responsible for imparting necessary technical know how to the tea growers have failed to serve the tea growers".

The tea scenario had undergone major changes in terms of area, productivity and ownership etc. due to many socio-economic factors. A need to update database was being realized for quite some time to formulate development strategies for the tea industry of Himachal Pradesh. An exhaustive survey of the entire area under tea in Himachal Pradesh was conducted by the Tea Board India and the Tea Directory of HP was published by the Assistant Director, Tea Board, Palampur in the year 1997. The Tea Directory provided valuable information regarding the number of tea growers, extent of area, production etc. and identified area under production, neglected area and the abandoned area. The information was valuable for formulating an action plan to revitalize the tea industry of Himachal Pradesh. A summary of the highlights of the survey is appended:

- A total number of 3679 tea growers represent an area under tea of 2312 hectare spread over four tehsils of Palampur, Baijnath, Kangra, Dharamshala in the district of Kangra and one each in Jogindernagar and Bhatyat in the districts of Mandi and Chamba, respectively.
- Tehsil Palampur covers the maximum area of 1256 hectare followed by Baijnath 564.4 hectares, Dharamshala 231.7 hectare, Jogindernagar 193.4 hectare, Kangra 65.49 hectare and lastly Bhatiyat with 0.98 hectare.

- Most significantly approximately 96 per cent of the total tea growers are having possession less that 2 hectare comprising 46.97 per cent of the total tea area while rest 53.03 per cent tea area are shared among 4 per cent of the tea growers only.
- Only 150 tea growers having possession of 444.9 hectare which comes to 4 per cent of the total tea growers are fully dependent on tea for their livelihood while 469.4 and 625 hectare fall under neglected and abandoned category, respectively, for various reasons like absentee landlords, lack of economic resources etc. There is also an area of 3572.15 hectare other than tea under the tea growers' possession.
- Based on the figure of 1996 the annual total made tea production stands as 14.23 lakh kg splitting Black and Green tea as 7.56 and 6.67 lakhs kg., respectively. Excluding the abandoned area the average yield in terms of made tea/ hectare stands as 843 kg. and optimum productivity was found to be 3000 kg. made tea/hectare.
- Apart from negligible private sale, most of the produce of Black & Green tea was sold at Calcutta and Amritsar with an average price of Rs. 54.55 and Rs. 32.51, respectively according to the sale report of 1996.
- Out of total produce of made tea 55 per cent & 45 per cent are manufactured in Cooperative and Private tea factories, respectively.

The State Government opened the office of Technical Officer Tea (TOT) with a view to provide all technical support to the tea industry. The department provided inputs like fencing materials, fertilizers, pesticide sprayers, planting material etc. on subsidy and other technical know-how. It also established a tea nursery of 2,50,000 plant capacity and provided tea saplings to the growers at a very nominal price. The Indo-German Dhauladhar Project, an integrated farm-forestry project engaged in improving the ecology and economy of this region also made sincere efforts to help the tea growers. National Bank for Agriculture and Rural Development (NABARD) extended support to the tea plantation by providing loans. The Government of Himachal Pradesh also provided financial support to the Cooperative Tea Factories and Marketing Society in the shape of managerial subsidy, interest rate subsidy and contribution to share capital from time to time. Government of India too helped the growth of tea industry by exempting excise duty on green tea.

In 1964 the State Government had established the first Cooperative Tea Factory at Bir (District Mandi). The factory had a capacity of manufacturing 1,00,000 kg. orthodox tea but, due to lack of quality tea manufacture expertise it switched over to green tea manufacture. A second Cooperative Tea Factory equipped with modern machinery was commissioned at Palampur (District Kangra) in 1980. The factory had a capacity to manufacture 5,00,000 kg. orthodox black tea per annum. A third and fourth Cooperative Tea Factories were established at Baijnath (District Kangra) in 1981 and at Sidhbari (District Kangra) in 1984, each with a capacity of manufacturing 2,00,000 kg. tea. Although the Cooperative Tea Factories provided remunerative prices to the growers for their green leaf supplies but, due to the poor quality of the raw material received, these tea factories failed to capture the lost market at Calcutta. Consequently these Cooperative Tea Factories were trapped into heavy accumulated losses.

Setting up of Tea Federation gave a boost to the development of tea gardens and tea factories. Organizing of the Kangra Tea Festival from 5-7 June, 1992 at Palampur by the State Government provided a platform to promote Kangra tea on National and International levels was a big success. Four brands of Kangra tea namely Darbari, Bageshwari, Bahar and Malhar were launched during the festival.

The cumulative efforts by all the agencies involved in R & D, extension and development succeeded, to some extent in reviving the tea industry of Himachal Pradesh. Increase in yield of green leaf was recorded, the annual production of made tea increased steadily from 6,77,000 kg. in 1985 to 17,11,000 kg. in 1998 (Fig. 1.1). The quality of made tea was also improved and so was its valuation. In 1991 the Palampur Cooperative Tea Factory Limited, Palampur was awarded Chairman's Challenge Trophy for quality tea production and also for highest all-India price (Rs. 300 per kg.) amongst the cooperative factories. This industry earned revenue for the State besides providing employment, directly or indirectly, to approximately 6000 workers. An area of about 7700 hectares has been identified as non-traditional area suitable for tea cultivation in the district of Chamba, Kangra and Mandi. However, the scenario of tea in Himachal Pradesh has not been encouraging at the beginning of the 21st century (Fig. 1.2).

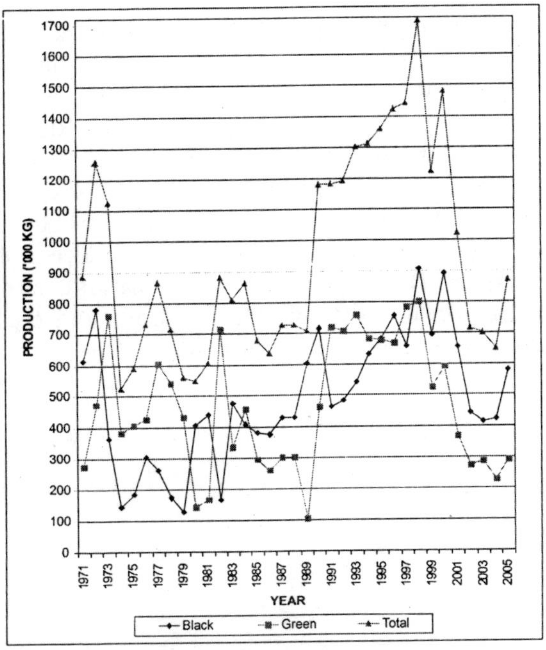

Fig. 1.1: Variations in the production of Tea (Black, Green and Total) in Himachal Pradesh since 1971

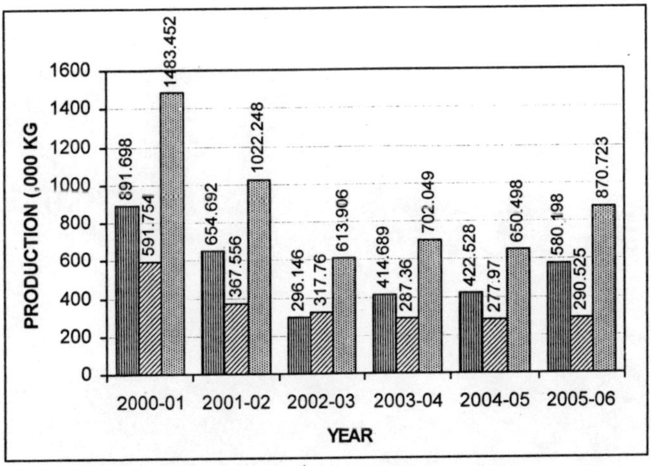

Fig. 1.2: Tea (Black, Green and Total) production in Himachal Pradesh from 2000 to 2005

The opening up of international trade due to the World Trade Organization (the WTO) Agreements has thrown a challenge; whereas the beginning of new Intellectual Property regime due to introduction of Trade Related Aspects of Intellectual Property Rights (TRIPS) Agreement from 1st January, 2005 has opened new avenues for the tea of Himachal Pradesh. Efforts to acquire Geographical Indications (GIs) status for Kangra tea have succeeded. Because of the climate of tea growing regions in Himachal Pradesh, the prevalence of diseases and pests is trivial. The use of synthetic chemicals is at its minimum. Hence the region is most suitable for producing organic tea. Diversification is also the need of the hour.

2

Research and Development *Agrotechnique Management and Extension*

Research work in the field is going on ever since the concept of cultivating tea in Kangra valley came into existence. Major Paske in his report offered the following remarks regarding the suitability of climate, soil and other conditions prevalent in the valley for the cultivation of tea as early as 1872 "As regards climate, a hot, damp climate, with a rainfall of not less than 100 inches per annum, is shown to be required for teas, and this climate the Kangra Valley possesses for at least seven months in the year, at elevations from 2,500 feet to 4,500 or 5,000 feet above the sea; nor within these elevations is the cold so severe during the remaining months of the year as in any way to injure or retard the growth of the tea-plant. The lowest elevation at which an estate is situated is 2,437 feet, and the highest elevation of any estate 5,500 feet. There is, however, only one estate at so high an elevation, the next highest is at 4,500 feet and the generality of the estates are at elevations between 3,000 and 4,000 feet. Hot winds are not known in the Kangra Valley, and between the months of March and October there is considerable moist heat, accompanied by a rainfall of, on the average, 110 inches in the year at Palampur. The great Dhaola Dhar or snow range on the slopes of which, or in the valley below, the tea estates are situated, besides apparently arresting the passage of clouds and causing them to exhaust their rain more copiously in the valley below, provides great facilities for irrigation in the numerous mountain streams and torrents fed from perennial snows. In the matter of soil while no artificial arrangements can alter the conditions of the climate, soil can be in measure created, and at any rate, considerably improved. With little artificial knowledge I possess on the subject of tea culture, I do not profess to know which is the best soil for teas. While some say that a rich, greasy loam, and others a light sandy loam, is the best soil, I observe that there are considerable varieties of soil on which tea has been planted in the District, and all these it has succeeded more or less, the measure of success of course depending much upon the extent of labour and pains and skill in cultivation. Connected with the question of soil comes the subject of manure. All the tea planters are well aware of the advantages of manure in increasing the yield of plants, and all avail themselves to some extent to think, however, that on the whole, planters might make greater efforts to increase their supplies of manure."

Two institutions namely the CSK Himachal Pradesh Krishi Vishvavidyalaya (CSKHPKV), Palampur and Institute of Himalayan Bioresource Technology (IHBT), Palampur have been involved in research and development in the field of tea. In each of them there is an independent department/division; in the CSKHPKV-Department of Tea Husbandry and Technology and in the IHBT-Hill Area Tea Science (HATS) Division, are taking care of the research and development activities on tea of this region. Raising of nurseries, plant improvement, agro-techniques for tea cultivation, doses and schedules of fertilizers' applications, green leaf yield, nutrient status of soil of tea gardens and green tea leaf, tea processing technology, rejuvenation of neglected or abandoned tea gardens, breeding of new varieties, product diversification etc. are the major area of research work.

2.1 CSK Himachal Pradesh Krishi Vishvavidyalaya (CSKHPKV), Palampur

The Tea Experiment Station (presently the Department of Tea Husbandry and Technology, CSKHPKV, Palampur) has been developing suitable agro-techniques to improve productivity of tea orchards in this region. The empirical results regarding agro-techniques, soil and plant nutrition management, disease control, pest management, rejuvenation techniques etc. have been translated into package of practices from time to time for the benefit of tea planters. China hybrid type of plant material has been found suitable due to its quality of resistance to pest and diseases and adaptation to the climatic conditions of this region.

Studies were conducted to ascertain reasons for low average yield,

843 kilogram made tea per hectare (KMTH^{-1}), of tea in Himachal Pradesh compared to the national average of 1948 KMTH^{-1}. Lack of tea garden management, inadequate soil fertility, lack of resources and lack of interest were identified to be due to the following reasons:

- 96 per cent of the 3679 tea growers occupy about 47 per cent of the total area of 2312 hectare had less than 2 hectare land holdings.
- Tea cultivation was major source of livelihood for only 4 per cent growers.
- About 469 hectare tea area was in total neglect.
- About 625 hectare tea area was abandoned due to absentee owners or other domestic reasons.
- Lack of nutrient supplementing resulted into poor productivity.

The multidisciplinary research work carried out by the CSKHPKV scientists has been compiled in "Tea Cultivation in Himachal Pradesh" by the Directorate of Extension Education, CSKHPKV, Palampur in the year 2000 for the benefit of the tea growers. Major recommendations were based on the observations recorded through consistent field and laboratory work for more than 30 years. Agro-techniques, nutrition management and application of manure, pruning and plucking cycles, high yielding clones and secured nursery plants availability, weed and insect-pest managements, plant protection and disease control, quality tea manufacture etc. suitable for tea cultivation and processing under the agro-climatic conditions of the region were developed. The ensuing salient findings and recommendations are presented in the following pages.

2.1.1 Climate and Soil

Factors affecting the climate are rainfall, temperature, relative humidity and wind. For optimum growth of tea, there seems no upper limit to rainfall, however, less than 1200 mm rainfall could prove deleterious for tea. Uniform production can be achieved employing irrigation during dry spell when the relative humidity ranges between 35–52 per cent. Easily crumbling, acidic soils (pH 4.5–6) with desirable carbon: nitrogen ratio 10:1 that are able to provide good depth is suitable for tea cultivation. The Department of Tea Husbandry and Technology, CSKHPKV, Palampur is one of the centers recognized by the Tea Board India for soil analysis.

2.1.2 Planting Material

Under the agro-climatic conditions of Kangra valley of Himachal Pradesh it is only the China type (*Camellia sinensis* L.) tea bushes found suitable for cultivation. Two new tea clones namely Kangra Asha (KVK-1) and Kangra Jwala (KVK-3) from the local selections were released in 1989, after monitoring their performance with respect to yield of green tea shoots, quality of tea etc. The main characters of these varieties are:

1. *Kangra Asha (KVK-1):* Vigorous and uniform growth, orthotropic, leaf pose semi-erect and dark green in colour, resistant to drought, frost and hails, market evaluation is very high.
2. *Kangra Jwala (KVK-3):* Uniform and vigourous growth, semi-orthotropic, leaf pose semi-erect, light green in colour. Tea has got wiry characters with very high market valuation.

The other recommended varieties are TV1, TV8, TV9 TV23, Phoobsering-312, Tukdah-253 and seed stock Nanda Devi.

2.1.3 Propagating Techniques

Propagation techniques from seeds and cuttings were standardized:

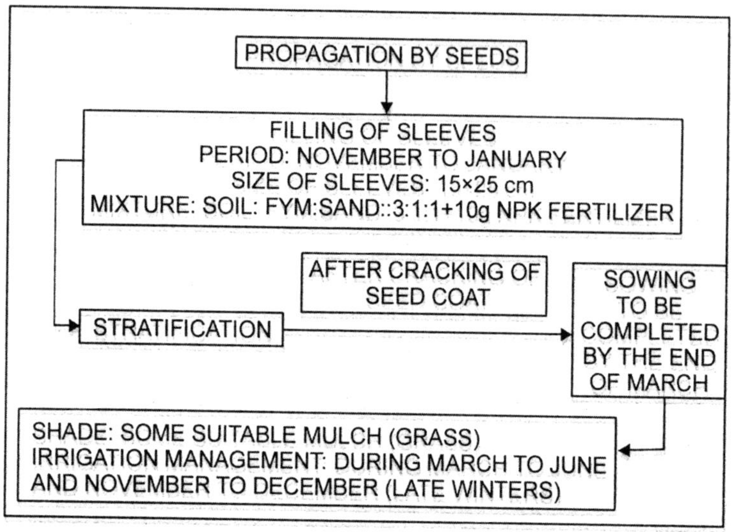

PROPAGATION BY CUTTINGS

MATERIAL: SINGLE LEAF INTER-NODAL SEMI-HARDWOOD WITH A DORMANT BUD IN AXIAL OF PENCIL THICKNESS

PLANTING TIME: JULY TO OCTOBER OR EVEN NOVEMBER
IDEAL TEMPERATURE: 21°C–25°C
IDEAL RELATIVE HUMIDITY: 80–90%

TRANSFER OF CUTTINGS INTO POLYTHENE SLEEVES: AFTER 4 MONTHS
HARDENING PROCESS; FOR A PERIOD OF 3-4 MONTHS PRIOR TO TRANSPLANTING IN THE FIELDS

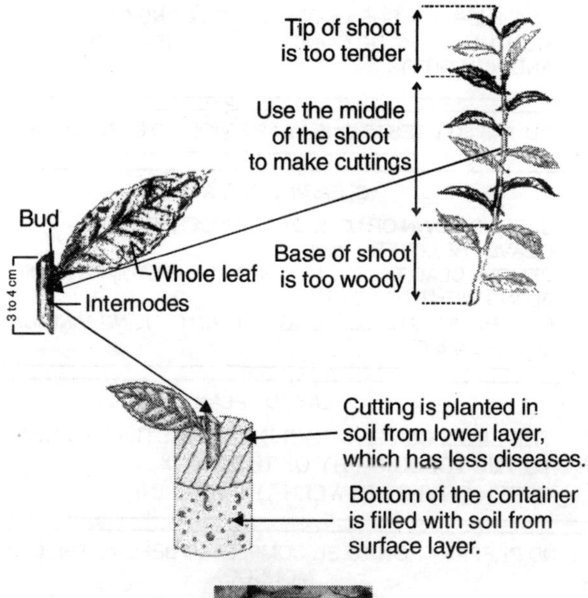

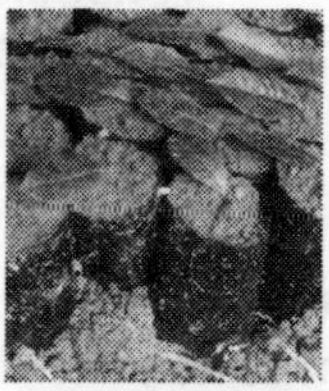

Cuttings Planted in Plastic Bags

Techniques to establish biclonal seed baries from plants of two different clones or varieties whose growth, yield and liquor characteristics were satisfactory and the progeny had a fair degree of morphological uniformity, were developed.

2.1.4 Land Preparation

Virgin forest land was recommended for tea growing and following steps were recommended for land preparation:

HISTORY OF THE AREA

- WHETHER IT CARRIED TEA IN THE PAST
- PRESENT VEGETATION
- PERIOD OF GRAZING/CULTIVATION
- WHETHER ANY BURNING HAS BEEN DONE ON THE SITE
- MONTHLY CLIMATIC CONDITIONS (RAINFALL, TEMPERATURE AND HUMIDITY)

SUITABILITY TESTS ONE YEAR PRIOR TO ESTABLISHMENT

CLEARING THE AREA

- CUTTING DOWN OR UPROOTING UNDERGROWTH (LEAVE THE LITTER *in situ*)
- REMOVE DEAD TREES AND UPROOT THE STUMPS COMPLETELY ALONG WITH ROOT SYSTEM
- FILL THE PITS AND LEVELING OF LAND CAUSING MINIMUM SOIL DISTURBANCE

LAYOUT PLAN

- THE LINES OF TEA SHOULD BE STRICTLY ACCORDING TO THE TOPOGRAPHY OF THE LAND
- GREEN COVER BETWEEN THE TEA LINES

LAND PREPARATION TO BE COMPLETED BEFORE THE ONSET OF MONSOON

2.1.5 Layout

In case of dwarf Chinery type tea bushes a some what closer spacing in the hedge row with plant density 14,000-20,000 bushes per hectare was advantageous for quick ground coverage, plucking point distribution and yield. Different systems of layout namely single hedge square or rectangular system, equilateral triangular system, staggered hedge system, contour system have been worked out.

2.1.6 Young Tea Plant Management

Under the conditions of Himachal Pradesh monsoon and even the autumn period was considered optimum for successful planting of tea. The winter and early spring rains following transplantation was found to be more useful for the establishment of young tea plants, however, transplantation during spring was not found to be successful. The planting techniques, weed control, pests and disease control, and frame formation techniques were standardized. Pruning operations for decentering are given in Table 2.1.

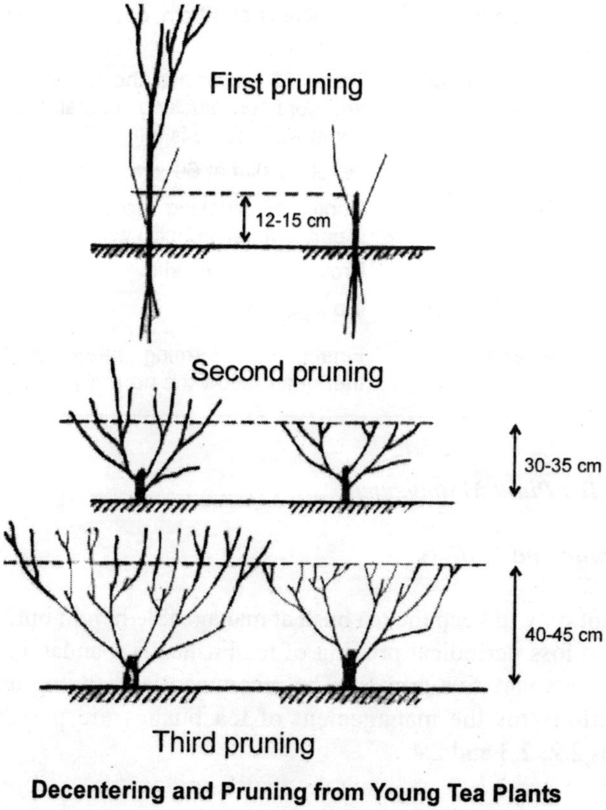

Decentering and Pruning from Young Tea Plants

Table 2.1: Recommended pruning operations for decentering

Age of plant (years)	*Month*	*Recommended Operations*
0	July–September	Plant tea in the field
1	April–August	Tip at 50 cm
	September	Decenter at 10-15 cm cut across laterals at 30 cm
2	April–June	Tip at 50 cm
	July–October	Continue plucking at 55 cm (raising by a leaf when table is full)
	December	Level off skiff at 60 cm
3	April–October	Pluck over janam approximately 62 cm (raising by a leaf when table is full)
	December	Cut across at 30 cm, decenter wherever necessary
4	April–October	Tip at 55 cm above the ground measure and continue plucking regularly raising by a leaf when table is full
	December	Level off skiff at 60 `cm
5	April–October	Continue plucking raising by a leaf (approximately 62 cm) when table is full
	December	Provide medium skiff
6	April–October	Tip at 60 cm
	December	Final frame forming prune at 35 cm, thereafter follow the normal pruning cycle

2.1.7 Tea Plant Management

A. Prune and Skiff

It is not only to keep the tea bush at manageable height but, in spite of crop loss periodical pruning of tea bushes is mandatory for the vigorous vegetative growth. The recommended pruning and skiff operations for the management of tea bushes are presented in Tables 2.2, 2.3 and 2.4.

Table 2.2: Pruning operation

Type of Pruning	*Purpose of Pruning*	*Extent of Pruning*	*Tipping Measure*
Collar prune or Heavy prune	To rejuvenate tea bush	0-20 cm from ground level	55 cm from ground level
Medium prune or cut back prune	Removal of unproductive wood and knots	35-50 cm from ground level	15-20 cm above prune level
Top prune or light prune	Removal of excessive knots	2-5 cm above previous pruning mark	

Table 2.3: Skiff operation

Type of Skiff	*Purpose of Skiff*	*Extent of Skiff*	*Tipping Measure*
Level off skiff	To level plucking table, removal of stubs and old leaf above the plucking surface	5 cm above the latest tipping level	
Light skiff	Removal of plucking points	At or within 1 cm of previous tipping level	Pluck to janam if the bush has adequate maintenance foliage
Medium skiff		5 cm below the last tipping level or 15 cm above previous pruning mark	At previous tipping level by leaving a minimum of one leaf on each newly developed primary.
Deep skiff		Midway between pruning and tipping levels or as recommended	New growth is tipped by leaving 3-4 leaves (7-10 cm) above the skiff and pluck janam

Table 2.4: Type of operation in pruning cycle

Year	*Type of operation*
0 (Pruned year)	Pruning
1	Level off skiff
2	Deep skiff
3	Level off skiff
4	Light prune and repeat the cycle
5	Light prune

B. Rejuvenation and Infilling

The recommended programmes of work to be carried out for the rejuvenation of old tea bushes and infilling in the rejuvenated sections along with periods and common herbicides for young tea plantation are presented in Tables 2.5, 2.6 and 2.7, respectively.

Table 2.5: Rejuvenation of old deteriorated tea bushes

Year	*Period (Month)*	*Programme of Work*
0	February-March	Apply N, P and K fertilizer mixture @ 90:90:40 kg/ha taking standing density into consideration.
	April-August	Pluck the tea bushes at regular intervals.
	September	Stop plucking and allow the bushes to grow so as to accumulate starch reserve in the roots.
	November-December	Cut out pruning operation from ground level to 20 cm height depending upon the condition of the bushes. Remove all dead, diseased and knotty branches. Leave the pruning material on the ground till the leaves have fallen.
1	January-February	After the completion of pruning carry out light hoeing near the periphery of the tea bushes and remove deep rooted grasses. Mix FYM in soil.
	May-June	Spray Glyphosate @ 2L in 500L water per hectare and repeat the same with reduced rate if necessary to control thatch grass.
	July-October	Apply NPK fertilizer @ 90:90:40 kg/ha in two splits during July and September. Tip the primary shoots at a height of 55 cm

(*Contd.*)

(Contd.)

Year	*Period (Month)*	*Programme of Work*
		from the ground taking care that nothing is removed from below the site.
	November-December	Level the regenerated tea bushes with hand.
2	February-March	Apply NPK @ 90:90:40kg/ha.
	April-June	Tip/pluck at 55cm from the ground level.
	July-October	Carry on plucking. Control weed and insect/pest in the plantation.
	November-December	Hand leveling/level off skiff.
3	February-March	Apply NPK @ 90:90:40kg/ha.
	April-June	Tip/pluck at 55cm from the ground level.
	July-October	Carry on plucking. Control weed and insect/pest in the plantation and carry on plucking.
	November-December	If the stem wood is sufficiently thick then cut back to 35cm from the ground level in order to establish the permanent frame.
4	February-March	Apply NPK @ 90:90:40kg/ha.

Table 2.6: Maintenance of infill in the rejuvenated sections

Year	*Period (Month)*	*Programme of Work*
0	February-July	Prepare pits of 30 ×45 cm size and plant one seedling per pit and allow it to grow freely during the year.
1	February-December	Apply 2:1:2 NPK mixtures to each plant and tip it at 60 cm during the season. Decentre it in between 20-30 cm during the month of December. Control weeds growth. Lope off branches of rejuvenates extending toward infill.
2	February-July	Apply 2:1:2 NPK mixtures to each plant and tip it at 60 cm.
	December	Level off skiff may be given to new infill.
3	February	Apply 2:1:2 NPK mixtures to each plant and keep on plucking at 60 cm throughout the growing season.
	December	Prune the infill bushes at 35 cm.
4	February	Apply NPK fertilizers @ 90:90:40 kg/ha infill as well as rejuvenated bushes.
5		Follow the normal pruning cycle along with old rejuvenated bushes.

Table 2.7: Common herbicides recommended for young tea plantation

Herbicide	*Dilution Rate*	*Spray Solution (L/ha)*
Gramoxane	1: 300	500
2,4-D	1: 400	400
Glyphosate	1: 200	400
Simazine	1: 100	500

2.1.8 Plant Protection

A. Insect-Pest

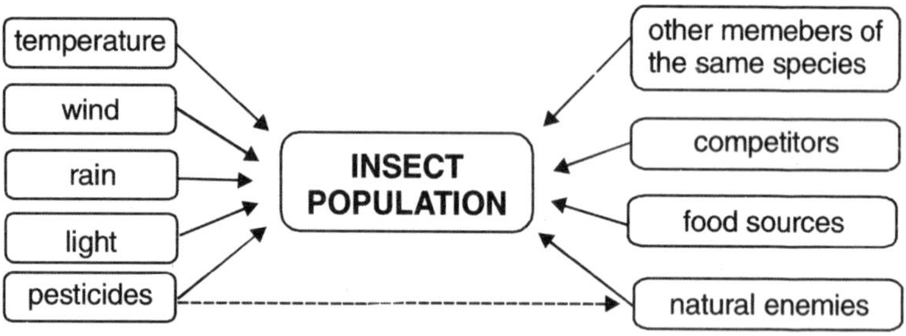

Physical and Biological Factors Responsible for Insect Population

Of the 300 plus species of arthropods the pests identified in tea growing regions of Kangra and Mandi are purple mite [*Calacarus carinatus* (green) Acarina], tea leaf folder [*Gracilaria theivora* Walson], tea thrips [*Scirtothrips dorsalis* Hood], tea aphid [*Toxoptera aurantii* Boyer], and leaf minor [*Tropiconytes theae* Cotes], mealy bug [*Pseudococcid sp.*], Jassids [*Emposea flavescens*].

Damage Caused by Mealy Bug

Damage Caused by Leafhopper

The tea plant protection from these pests has been standardized. The period of infestation, foliar symptoms of insect-pest infestation and recommended control measures on the appearance of symptoms are given in Table 2.8.

Table 2.8: Period of infestation, symptoms and control of insect-pest in tea

Insect-Pest	*Infestation Period*	*Symptoms*	*Control*
Purple mite	April-July	Copperish discolouration on upper surface	Dicofol (Kelthane 18.5 EC) @2025 ml or Ethion (Miticil 50 EC) @ 1500 ml or Neemark-Achook @ 2250 ml/ 750 L of water/ha (Repeat after 15 day interval if necessary)
Tea thrips	March-July	Large number of brown streaks. Leaf surface becomes uneven, curled and matty.	Endosulfan (Thiodan 35 EC) @ 1500 ml or Neemark-Achook @ 2250 ml/750 L of water/ha.
Leaf folder	July-September	Leaf rolls from tip downward and folds inside.	Remove infested leaves. Endosuelfan (Thiodan-35 EC) @ 1500 ml or Decamethrin (Decis 2.8 EC @ 675 ml + Bt (Dipol 8 L) @ 1125 ml/750 L of water/ha. (Repeat after 15-20 day interval)
Tea aphids	June-October	Dark brown aphid colonies on tender shoots. Leaf curls.	Spray Endosulfan (Thiodan-35 EC) @ 1500 ml or Malathion (Cythion 50 EC @ 1500 ml/750 L of water/ha.
Mealy bug	March-August	Crawling nymphs, white body moulding on lower leaves and sooty mould development.	Decamethrin (Decis) @ 0.05%
Jassids	May-August	Short holes form on tender shoots and leaves.	Spray Endosulfan (Thiodan-35 EC) @ 1500 ml/750 L of water/ha

B. Diseases

Blister blight caused by *Exonbasidium vexans* Massee is the most destructive disease of tea [*Camellia sinensis* (L) O Kuntze]. The disease is known to occur in almost all tea growing areas. The cool and humid climate of tea growing regions of Himachal Pradesh is favourable to the pathogens to spread the disease which attains an epidemic like condition during monsoon season leading to severe crop loss. Blister blight in tea of Himachal Pradesh was first recorded in 1968-69 by Saharan and Chouhan; during the monsoon season of 1986, the disease appeared in an epidemic form in most of the tea plantations. Most tea diseases are caused by fungi, but bacteria, algae, virus and other biotic agents also attack the tea bushes. The foliar symptoms of diseases and recommended controls along with pathogens and symptoms are presented in Table 2.9.

Table 2.9: Symptoms and control of diseases in tea

Disease/ Pathogen	*Symptoms*	*Control Measures*
Blister blight/ *Exobasidium vexans* Massee	Blister with whitish mass on pluckable shoots with the onset of rainy season during July to October.	Callixin (Tridemorph 80% EC) @ 0.2% or Contaf (Hexacaonazole 5% EC) @ 0.1% at 15 day interval followed by Blitox (Copper oxychloride 50% WP) @ 0.3% at 7 day interval alternatively.
Brown blight/ *Colletotrichum camellia*	Yellowish to chocolate brown patches on mature leaves.	Dithane M-45 @0.3% at 7-10 day interval on affected bushes.
Grey blight/ *Pestalotia*	Light to dark-brown patches with grayish centre on mature leaves	Dithane M-45 @0.3% at 7-10 day interval on affected bushes.
Red rust/ *Cephaleuros mycoidea*	Brick-red or orange rusty spots which ultimately coalesce to each other to form large spots on stem and leaves of tea uhes.	Bordeaux mixture or Dithane M-45 @ 0.3% at 7-10 day interval.

(*Contd.*)

(*Contd.*)

Disease/ Pathogen	*Symptoms*	*Control Measures*
Brown root rot/ *Fomes noxius*	Affected tea bush leaves wither initially and the bush dies later on.	Senitation: Uproot and destroy the affected bushes.
Charcoal stump rot/ *Ustulina deusta*	Brittle black encrustation with fan-shaped film underneath the bark of affected roots.	Fumigation: Methyl bromide or formalin should be applied in the affected regions. Drainage: Arrangements for proper draining of water.

2.1.9 Extension Activities

The Department of Tea Husbandry and Technology, CSKHPKV, Palampur is also actively involved in extension activities:

(*a*) Making available elite plant materials to the planters through the development agencies.

(*b*) Transfer of technology through adaptive research trials, direct contact with the planters, radio and television talks, publications and training programmes etc.

(*c*) Organizing field days either at the adaptive research trial sites or at the experimental fields of the department.

(*d*) Organizing training programmes on the techniques of tea cultivation for the officers of the Department of Agriculture, Government of Himachal Pradesh, industry and field workers.

An area of about 60 acres under the thick thorny bushes that was abandoned tea garden since 1960s was rejuvenated and developed into an income generating tea garden and is a living example of the application of the technology developed at the CSKHPKV, Palampur by the interdisciplinary integrated efforts of research of the scientists, hardwork and toil of the tea workers and management. The Department of Tea Husbandry and Technology has brought out versatile guidelines in the form of a Calendar of Tea Operations.

Himachal Pradesh Krishvishvavidyalaya Palampur
Department of Tea Husbandry and Technology

Calendar of Operations in Tea

January

Tea Nursery

- Place sand and seed in alternate layers for stratification.
- Fill up sleeves with soil, sand and FYM mixture (3:1:1).
- Provide watering.
- Transfer callused cutting into sleeves.

Young Tea

- Deenter at 7-10 cm from ground and cut across at 30-35 cm.
- Apply NPK (Nitrogen, Phosphorus, Potassium) (2:1:2) fertilizer mixture as per age of plant.

Mature Tea

- Carry out collar (0-20 cm from ground) or medium-top pruning (35 cm from ground or 5 cm above last pruning mark).

February

Tea Nursery

- Sow seeds in sleeves 1 cm deep, provide mulch and watering.
- Transfer callused cuttings into sleeves.

Young Tea

- As in January, where necessary.

Mature Tea

- Continue collar-medium pruning up to first fortnight.
- Apply NPK fertilizer mixture @ 90:90:40 kg/ha.

March

Tea Nursery

- Seed sowing activates.
- Transfer of cuttings.
- Apply NPK (2:1:2) fertilizer mixture @ 20 kg/ha to one year old nursery.
- Provide overhead shade using nylon nets/coir mat or suitable material.

Young Tea

- Sow temporary-shade species such as Crotalaria, Tephrosia, Leucaena, Rubinia etc.
- Apply 2:1:2 NPK fertilizer mixture in splits of recommended dose.

Mature Tea

- Mix fertilizers by forking in moist soil.
- Spray zinc @ 1.25 kg/ha in 500 L. water control mites using dicofol (Kelthane 18.5 EC) @ 2025 ml or Ethion (Miticil 50 EC) @ 1500 ml/750 L water.
- Control mealy bugs by Decamethrin (Decis 2.8 EC) @ 1340 ml or Endosulfan (Thiodon 35 EC) @ 1500 ml or Neemark/Achook @ 2250 ml/750 L water.
- Tip tender shoots from un-pruned sections.

April

Tea Nursery

- Arrange proper over-head shade.
- Apply fertilizer mixture (10 kg SOA (Sulphate of ammonia), 6.5 kg SSP (Single super phosphate) and 3.5 kg MOP (Muriate of potash)/ha) to one year old nursery plants.
- Carry out hand weeding in tea nursery.
- Provide irrigation.

Young Tea

- Apply NPK (2:1:2) fertilizer mixture as per age.
- Provide irrigation.

Mature Tea

- Pluck tea bushes at 6-7 days interval above skiffing level.
- Spray dicofol (Kelthane 18.5 EC) @ 2025 ml or Ethion (Miticil 50 EC) @ 1500 ml in 750 L water to control mites.
- For mealy-bug control spray Decamethrin (Decis 2.8 EC) @ 1340 ml or Endosulfan (Thiodon 35 EC) @ 1500 ml or Neemark/Achoock @ 2250 ml in 750 L water, immediately after plucking round. Repeat spray at 15-20 days interval.

May

Tea Nursery

- Hand weeding in tea nursery.
- Provide irrigation.
- Maintain proper shade.

Young Tea

- Tip young tea at 55 cm and continue plucking
- Provide irrigation.
- Maintain adequate temporary shade such as *Crotalaria anagyroides*, Leucaena and Rubinia in young tea, planted 2 m × 2 m spacing initially and 4 m × 4 m at later stage.
- Control mites, thrips, leaf roller, aphids, jassids etc., by using recommended pesticides.

Mature Tea

- Pluck mature tea plantations at 7-9 days interval.

June

Tea Nursery

- Maintain proper shade and humidity.

- Follow hardening process of clonal nursery plants by opening polythene sheets occasionally towards northern side avoiding exposure to southern/western sides.

Young Tea

- Control insect-pest using recommended pesticides.
- Fill up the pits/trenches dug for new plantings by mixing. FYM (2-3 kg), super phosphate (25-30 g) and Folidol dust 10 g per plant basis.

Mature Tea

- Maintain shade in planted sections and provide irrigation.
- Pluck at 8-10 days interval above the janam.
- Tip the collar pruned bushes at 55 cm and medium/top pruned 15-20 cm above pruning mark.
- Control weeds by using Glyphosate @ 2 liters/ha followed by Oxyfluorfen @ 625 ml/ha after 10-15 days interval.
- Control mites, Jassids, beetles etc., in regenerated pruned sections, using recommended pesticides.

July

Tea Nursery

- Raise clonal nursery by using semi-hard wood, single leaf inter-nodal cuttings.
- Apply fertilizer mixture in 1 or 2 years old tea nurseries @ 10 kg sulphate of ammonia, 6.5 kg single super phosphate and 3.5 kg muriate of potash/ha per round of application.
- Thin out shade in nurseries and follow hardening of plants.

Young Tea

- Carry out transplanting in new areas.
- Follow cheeling.
- Raise green manuring crops such as cowpea, Crotalaria, Napier grass, Lemon grass etc., in areas proposed for new planting/replanting.

Mature Tea

- Continue plucking leaving adequate margin 15-20 cm above pruning marks for medium pruned bushes.
- Spray zinc @ 1.25 kg in 500 L water.
- Thin out excess shade to penetrate 50 per cent sun light.
- Adopt recommended weed management practices. Cut Lantana and Eupatorium 7-10 cm from ground level and allow them to regenerate. For monocot/dictol weeds use Glyphosate @ 2L/ha followed by Oxyfluorfen @ 625 ml/ha.
- Follow pest control management schedules (aphids, jassids, flush worms) by using Endosulfan (Thiodan 35EC) @ 1500 ml or Neemark/Achook @ 2250 ml/750 L water.
- Observe the incidence for blister blight, apply prophylactic spray of Calixin @ 0.2 per cent.
- Adopt proper drainage in tea areas.
- Carry out in filling/inter-planting in rejuvenated sections.

August

Tea Nursery

- Continue clonal propagation.
- Apply fertilizer mixture in 1 year old nurseries @ 10 kg. SOA, 6.5 kg SSP and 3.5 kg MOP/ha per round.
- Hand weeding.

Young Tea

- Continue transplanting.
- Mulch basins.

Mature Tea

- Do lopping of side branches of old bushes near the infills.
- Thin out excessive shade to penetrate 50 per cent sunlight.
- Continue in-filling/inter-planting.
- Spray regenerated Lantana and Eupatorium weeds with Glyphosate @ 4 ml/L.

- Adopt plant protection measures, i.e. insect-pests and blister blight.
- Stop plucking in areas proposed for rejuvenation, use herbicides and apply 2:1:2 NPK fertilizer mixture.

September

Tea Nursery

- Continue clonal propagation.
- Apply fertilizer mixture in nursery.

Young Tea

- Continue transplanting and mulch basins.
- Control aphids, leaf rollers and blister blight by using recommended insecticides/fungicides.
- Adopt recommended weed control measures.

Mature Tea

- Continue plucking at weekly interval.
- Spray Zinc @ 1.25 kg/ha in 500 L water.

October

Tea Nursery

- Continue clonal propagation.

Young Tea

- Plough the green manuring crops in the filed.

Mature Tea

- Continue plucking at 8-10 days interval.
- Follow plant protection measures.

November

Tea Nursery

- Collect the seed from seed barries and test their viability by floating test and store in dry and cool place.

Young Tea

- Follow centering and maintain basins of young plants.

Mature Tea

- Clear the area from thorny bushes/weeds.
- Carry out skiffing operations based on the age from pruning.
- Carry out the pruning in the proposed area.
- Follow hoeing in the pruned sections and burry the pruning litter.
- Adopt collar pruning in proposed areas for rejuvenation. Apply FYM and follow hoeing.

December

Tea Nursery

- Put seeds for stratification in alternate layers of seed and sand. Mulch beds and maintain moisture.

Young Tea

- Prepare layout plans for new plantations.
- Carry out pit digging/trenching operations.
- Decenter young tea section at 7-10 cm from ground if stem is 1 cm in thickness.

Mature Tea

- Remove excessive shade by lopping tree branches.
- Adopt collar pruning in proposed areas for rejuvenation, apply FYM and follow hoeing.

2.2 Institute of Himalayan Bioresource Technology (IHBT), Palampur

Major activities at the Institute of Himalayan Bioresource Technology (IHBT), Palampur, through its Hill Area Tea Science (HATS) Division include:

(i) Tea Husbandry

- Development of elite planting material
- Nursery Management
- Re-planting and rejuvenation of old and abandoned tea gardens
- Young tea management
- Weed Management
- Plant nutrition
- Organic farming
- Tea farm mechanization

(ii) Tea Processing

- Quality improvement through improved processing techniques
  (Stepping up chemical wither and time management for black tea manufacture)
- Product diversification

(iii) Entomology

- Pesticide residuc analysis
- Screening and testing of active molecules

(iv) Pathology

- Tea diseases of fungal origin
- Molecular basis of blister blight susceptibility and resistance

2.2.1 Elite Planting Material and Young Tea Management

The development, evaluation and maintenance of elite planting material were started in 1986 with the aim to:

- collect and evaluate tea germplasm
- introduce tea clones and biclonal seed-stocks from different tea growing regions
- select and evaluate promising tea strains amongst heterogeneous population in Kangra tea plantation
- hybridize among selected strains for specific characters
- evaluate new progenies for yield, quality and stress tolerance

In order to develop elite planting material rooting tests were performed on 12 TV series from North-East India and selections from local and institute's own tea gardens. In a field trial involving 86 clones and 4 seed stocks; the Happy Valley-39, TV-18, AV-2, UPASI-9 and Craigmore-6017 clones performed consistently better over a period of 3 to 5 years. Assessments on the quality parameters of made black tea indicated that St-449 and UPASI-9 had higher values for total polyphenols and catechin; UPASI-9 had higher values for theaflavin, thearubigin and caffeine while the clones Tukdah-78 and Phoobsering-312 had higher aroma notes. Biclonal seed stocks from North-East (TS-378, TS-450, TS-463) and South (BSS-1, BSS-3) India had survival percentage of 77-86 which was comparable to the local seed plants.

2.2.2 Breeding

The field performance of biclonal seed-stock BSS 1 and BSS 3: United Planters' Association of South India—Tea Research Foundation (UPASI-TRF) release, TS 449: Tea Research Association (TRA) release and of the clones B 157 and Tukdah 78 were better compared to the local China hybrid tea. Ambari a Darjeeling clone recorded the highest yield among the mature tea during the pruned year. Artificial pollination was carried out with a view to improve yield, quality and blister blight resistance in tea (Tables 2.10, 2.11).

2.2.3 Nursery

High yielding and drought resistant clones: KVK-1, UPASI-9 and UPASI-10 with high rooting performance were identified as ideal rootstocks. Composite plants were raised by cleft-grafting single node scions onto single node rootstock cuttings. Nursery performance of 65 accessions of Kangra *jat* origin was studied.

Table 2.10: Crosses made among the selected parents for tea improvement

Genotype	*B-157*	*T-383*	*UPASI-9*	*UPASI-10*	*T-78*	*CEF-2*	*KVK-1*	*Kopati*	*TV-1*	*SA-6*	*BS-26*	*Total*
KVK-1	155	263	255	125	125	203	—	—	—	—	—	1126
UPASI-10	—	—	261	—	—	279	340	134	280	—	—	1294
UPASI-9	232	219	—	106	92	318	75	169	211	240	—	1662
T-78	70	115	—	—	—	55	—	60	225	215	—	740
SA-6	—	—	—	303	—	—	278	—	—	—	330	911
TV-1	—	—	65	—	—	—	—	—	—	—	—	65
Total	457	597	581	534	217	855	693	363	716	455	330	5798

Table 2.11: Crosses among selected parents

Female ⇨ *Male* ⇩	*SA 6*	*UPASI 10*	*Tukdah 78*	*UPASI 3*	*UPASI 9*
Asha	325	273			
BS 55	221				
UPASI 10	273		297		
SA 6		149			
UPASI 3			156		128
UPASI 9			240	317	
BB 668			167		212
Tukdah 383			195		235
B 157			110		461
P 312					205
Tukdah 78					388
Tukdah 145					277
Kopati 1/1					63
CEF 02					213

An early flushing local selection, CEF-2 showed 77 per cent survival rate of its single node cuttings and growth vigour (average plant height: 17.5 cm and 9 leaves) that was comparable to the high yielding China hybrid clone AV-02. Cuttings of 12 TV series clones, four garden series clones and one tetraploid clone along with TRA biclonal seed stock materials were procured and planted in polytunnel for rooting. Morphological characterization of the 47 germplasm accessions maintained at Tea Experiment Farm, Banuri were carried out as per descriptors and incorporated in the tea database.

The capsules containing seeds of the crosses were screened for floaters and cracked in sterile, moist sand and sown in polybags which was kept in nursery for germination and further growth.

2.2.4 Taking Tea to the Non-traditional Area of Himachal Pradesh

In order to increase the area under tea in Himachal Pradesh a project was initiated in 1997 with the objective:

- to introduce tea in the non-traditional tea area of Himachal Pradesh.
- to popularize tea cultivation in the area within Kangra district where the returns from fruit and/or cereal crops were uncertain.

- to regenerate holistic eco-environment in the otherwise wasteland.

Tea bushes were planted in six selected (on the basis of suitable soil pH) plots in three districts namely Kangra (Peera in Changar), Mandi (Chail Chowk and Chogan) and Chamba (Khanora, Garnota and Bhangiana around Sihunta) of Himachal Pradesh. The performance of these plants at Khanora and Chogan was better compared to other areas. Severe drought during the summer months of 1999-2000 led to the discontinuation of tea culture at Peera in Changar, district of Kangra and Bangiana in district Chamba. Tea was also planted in Goomber area near Jwalamukhi in district Kangra.

2.2.5 Rejuvenation of Abandoned Tea Gardens

The development of abandoned/neglected gardens at Baijnath–44.43 acres, Bir–20 acres, Dharamshala–75 acres and at Palampur–10.57 acres to the profitable level was undertaken with the aim to motivate the tea growers to take up the development activities of other gardens lying in similar state that amount to about 47.3 per cent of the total area under tea cultivation in Himachal Pradesh. 27.39 acres of abandoned/neglected tea area was rejuvenated during 1997-98 and the remaining 122.61 acres of tea area belonging to 30 planters was selected and pruned for rejuvenation during 1998-99. Follow up actions were monitored during 1999-2001. The gardens productivity from 1999 to 2001 increased substantially Table 2.12.

Table 2.12: Crop production of abandoned/neglected tea gardens

		Yield KMTH^{-1} (Kilogram Made Tea Per Hectare)		
Zone	*Area*	*1999*	*2000*	*2001*
Baijnath	41.5	2,051	10,903	6,236*
Palampur	8.24	3,650	6,549	6,928
Dharamshala	81.3	4,988	20,293	17,680**

* Plots plucked up to April and August, 2001.

** Plots plucked up to July, 2001.

2.2.6 Pesticide Residue Studies

Detailed studies on "pesticides residue and metabolism in tea" were conducted on green tea shoots harvested at different intervals, made black tea and tea brew with the following objectives:

- To study the residues and metabolism of some pesticides used in tea plantation.
- To find the levels of residues after 7 and 14 days from the time of spray in green leaves, made tea and brew.
- To study the pattern of degradation of pesticides in soil and plants.
- To find out the metabolites and how they are affecting the total Maximum Recommended Limit (MRL).
- To find out LD_{50} for various chemicals.

Quinalphos and Dicofol

At 7th day, the residues in made tea were higher than their prescribed MRL levels. The infusion had these chemicals within prescribed limit. Similar results were obtained for methylparathion and chlorpyrifos. Progressive loss in quinalfos residue was observed during different stages (withering, rolling, fermentation and drying) of tea manufacture.

Deltamethrin, Cypermethrin, Glyphosate, 2, 4-D, Acephate and Hexacanazole

Residues of deltamethrin and cypermethrin in made tea were lower than their prescribed MRL levels after seven days of application. Glyphosate and 2, 4-D persisted in soil samples up to 10 days from application but, no residues were found in leaves. The residues of acephate were above MRL levels on 7th day.

Heat inactivation in case of green tea manufacture resulted larger losses of dimethoate, methylparathion, endosulfan, dicofol and deltamethrin pesticides compared to withering in the black tea manufacture. However, the loss of residues was dependent upon the physico-chemical nature of the pesticides. Increase in brewing time also increased the transfer of pesticides into the brew.

Contaf 5E Fungicide, Starthene 75SP Insecticide, Omite 57E Miticide and Fenazaquin 10E Miticide

The residue in made tea for omite 57E was below the prescribed MRL level after 7 days spray, however, the residues of contaf 5E, starthene

75SP and fenazquin 10E were found to be above the MRL level. Infusions of the tea, manufactured from green tea shoots plucked nine days after spraying were found to be safe in all cases except starthene 75SP.

Propargite, Fenazaquin and Diofol (new/improved)

The residues of fenazaquin and dicofol (new/improved) in infusion were below detection limit after 7 days of spraying whereas in case of propargite the infusion was free of pesticide after 9 days of application.

2.2.7 Disease Management

Assessment of variability and resistance against blister blight pathogen (*Exobasidium vexans* Massee) a destructive disease of tea was conducted with the following objectives:

- Identification and cataloguing of clones/seed stocks for resistance to blister blight.
- Assessment of variability in blister blight pathogen.
- Ultrastructure of host-parasite relationship, and pathogenesis related proteins and their function in defense mechanism.

One hundred and twelve accessions were tested against mixed pathogen populations. Accessions were assigned to seven categories from immune to highly susceptible, based on disease response. Four clonal half-sibs which exhibited resistance against four isolates of blister blight were identified from Kangra tea plantations and protein profiles of healthy and diseased leaves were quantified.

2.2.8 Organic Tea Farming

Studies on organic tea farming were initiated in 1991 with the following objectives:

- To compare the efficacy of certain organic mulches and manures, smother crops and *in-situ* of organic mulch in terms of weed management.

- to evaluate the influence of organic mulching and manure on soil-fertility and plant nutrient management.
- to assess the influence of organic mulching and manure on yield and quality of made tea.
- to study the economics of organic tea production.

Indigenous plants namely *Imperata cylindrica, Lantana camara, Eupatorium conyzoides, Tagetes minuta, Grevillea robusta, Sesbania aegyptiaca* materials were employed for mulch along with farm yard manure (FYM) and humic acid. The treatment of FYM with *Lantana camara* as mulch recorded the highest yield followed by FYM with *Imperata cylindrica* over control. Tea leaf from the plots treated with FYM and humic acid had significantly high amounts of polyphenols and catechins and the liquor was reported to contain higher amounts of TF, TR and caffeine. No difference in the flavour profile of made tea was reported.

2.2.9 Product Diversification

Efforts were initiated to standardize optimum processing steps in the manufacture of green tea. Of the various techniques employed for the enzymes inactivation, use of microwave energy for inactivation and drying yielded better quality tea. The infusions of green teas manufactured following microwave inactivation and bi-directional rolling recorded higher levels of catechins compared to infusion of the teas manufactured by steam inactivation. Bi-directional rolling and roasting and unidirectional rolling recorded the lowest levels of catechins. Green and black tea based Ready-to-drink (RTD) tea formulations were developed. Improved method for making tea based wines from Himalayan wild flora was evolved and some high value, nutritive, herbal health wines were prepared. The organoleptic tasting revealed the unique characters of these wines which were similar to fresh wines acclaimed internationally. Fractionations through a number of solvent systems were carried out to isolate well defined groups of compounds having therapeutic values from tea. Studies to characterize the major constituents in Kangra valley tea responsible for its unique aroma/flavour are being undertaken in IHBT laboratories. The Kangra tea has shown the highest glycosidic precursors during the first flush and backend flush.

2.2.10 Patents

Table 2.13 List of Patents Filed/Secured by IHBT

No.	*Title*	*Filed Date*	*Country*	*Grant Date Month/day/ year*	*Patent No.*
1.	Cloning of novel gene sequences expressed and repressed during winter dormancy in the apical buds of tea (*Camellia sinensis* L (O Kuntze) bush	03/30/2001 03/30/2001 03/30/2001 04/06/2001 04/08/2005 04/08/2005 04/08/2005	CHINA SRI LANKA USA KENYA CHINA CHINA CHINA		
2.	An efficient method for microproduction of tea (*Camellia sinensis*) plants from leaf explants	03/14/2001 03/23/2001 03/23/2001 03/22/2001	SRI LANKA CHINA USA KENYA	04/28/2003 06/15/2005 07/29/2003	12368 ZL 01109920. 8 6599743
3.	An efficient one step method for micro-production of tea leaves	03/14/2001 03/20/2001 03/20/2001 03/20/2001	SRI LANKA CHINA USA KENYA	04/28/2003 04/15/2003	12369 6548300
4.	Tea leaf extract as a potent bactericidal agent for *Agrobacterium tumefaciens* mediated genetic transformations	04/06/2001	USA	07/06/2004	PP15080
5.	Cloning of 3 novel genes modulated under drought stress conditions in tea (*Camellia sinensis* L. (O.) Kuntze)	04/27/2002 03/28/2002 09/28/2004 09/28/2004 09/28/2004 09/29/2004 11/23/2004	USA PCT JAPAN KENYA MW SRI LANKA CHINA		
6.	Substitute of acetosyringone-A thermolabile caffeine fraction of tea leaves	03/25/2003 09/27/2004 09/27/2004 09/27/2004 09/27/2004 09/27/2004 11/24/2004 03/25/2003	USA KENYA JAPAN AUSTRALIA SRI LANKA BRAZIL CHINA PCT		

(*Contd.*)

(*Contd.*)

No.	Title	Filed Date	Country	Grant Date Month/day/ year	Patent No.
7.	A method for biolistic mediated genetic transformation of tea (*Camellia sinensis* L. (O.) Kuntze) using leaf explants	12/10/2001 07/21/2004 07/22/2004 07/22/2004 08/27/2004	USA KENYA SRI LANKA JAPAN CHINA		
8.	An improved method of tea propagation	01/20/1998 12/11/1997	KENYA SRI LANKA	07/05/2000 02/25/200	KE103 11355
9.	A mobile tea shoot preconditioning device for withering during black tea manufacture	02/02/2005 14/09/2005 19/09/2005	INDIA BANGLADE SH CHINA		
10.	Novel genes from drought stress tolerant tea plant a method (*Camellia Sinensis* (L) O. Kuntz)	09/06/2004	INDIA		
11.	Use of tea leaf extract as a potent bactericidal agent for *agrobacterium tumefacienns* mediated genetic transformations	08/13/2004 03/26/2002 03/27/2002	INDIA PCT USA		
12.	Transgenic tea through bilistic using leaf explants	07/22/2004 01/21/2003	INDIA PCT		
13.	A jacket attachment for carrying portable skiffing and shoot harvesting machines	02/11/2005	INDIA		
14.	Use of tea leaf extract for field inhibiting microbial transformant	03/14/2003 03/19/2003	SRI LANKA KENYA	06/30/2004	13019

3

Research and Development *Nutrients, Quality and Breeding*

3.1 Nutrient Status

The average yield of 825 kilogram made tea per hectare ($KMTH^{-1}$) in Himachal Pradesh is low compared to the national average of 1948 $KMTH^{-1}$ for which poor management of tea gardens with respect to nutrition was envisaged as one of the probable reasons. Considerable amounts of nutrients are removed from the soil through green tea shoots harvesting every year. A systematic study to assess the nutrient status of tea gardens of Himachal Pradesh under different management practices vis-à-vis well managed and poorly managed was carried out in order to facilitate the replenishment of these nutrients in tea gardens (Gagnesh *et al.* 2001). The results of these studies are given in Figures 3.1 to 3.4. In the factory zone-I (Palampur) that covers maximum area of 1256 hectare under tea the fertility of well managed gardens varied from medium to high status with respect to Nitrogen (N), Phosphorus (P), Potassium (K) and organic carbon. Magnesium (Mg) and Sulphur (S) contents were found to be deficient in 90-95 per cent and 10 per cent soil samples, respectively. Zinc (Zn) and copper (Cu) contents were deficient in 52-76 per cent tea soils. However, in tea shoots these nutrients were reported to be in medium class. Manganese (Mn) was reported to be in sufficient amount in both soils and tea shoots. On the basis of data thus collected it was observed that planters need to use additional dose of N, P, K, S and Zn with the recommended dose 90, 90, 90 of N, P, K fertilizer. Application of magnesium based micronutrient formulations and dolomite in both types of gardens were also suggested for balanced nutrition management. It was of interest to note that poorly managed tea gardens had good fertility status which could be due to lesser green leaf production. Follow up of recommended management and cultural practices were advocated for these gardens for higher green leaf production.

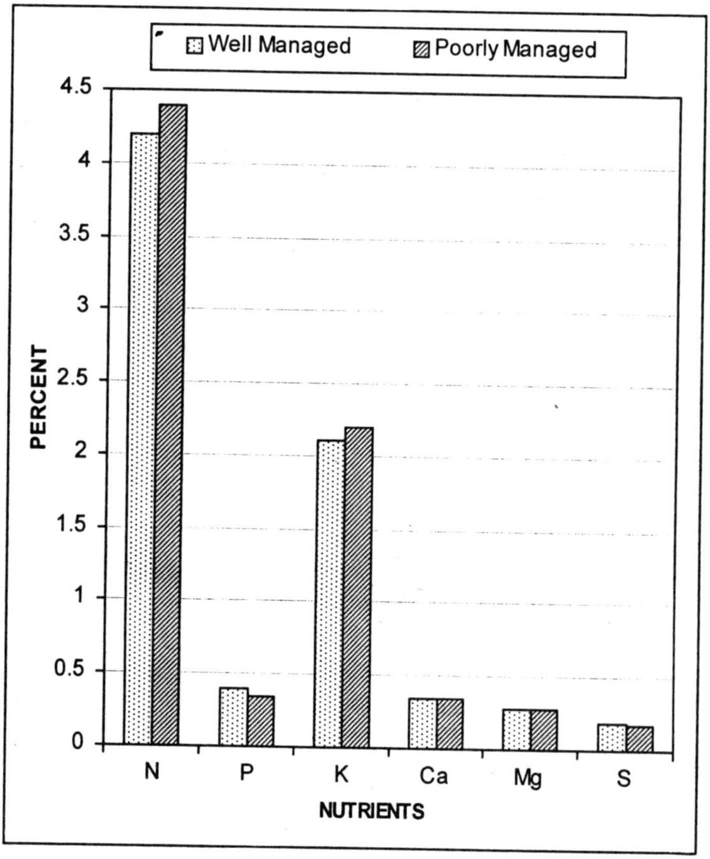

Fig. 3.1: Mean Nitrogen (N), Phosphorus (P), Potassium (K), Calcium (Ca), Magnesium (Mg) and Sulphur (S) contents in tea shoots of zone-I of Himachal Pradesh

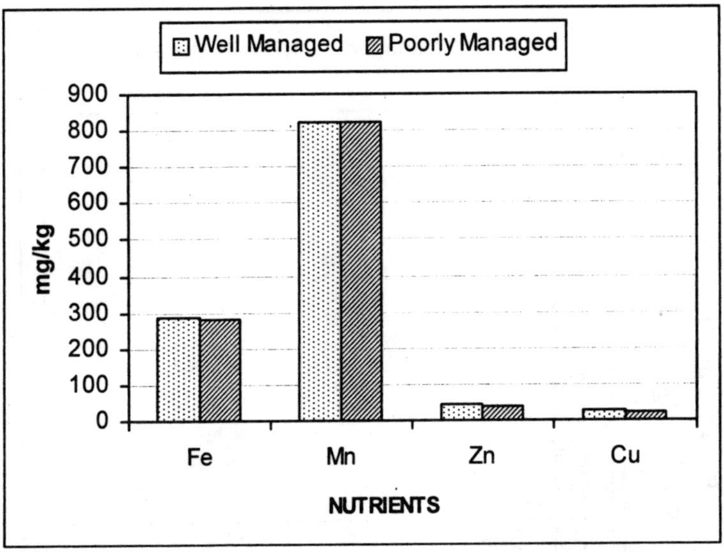

Fig. 3.2: Mean Iron (Fe), Manganese (Mn), Zinc (Zn) and Copper (Cu) contents in tea shoots of zone-I of Himachal Pradesh

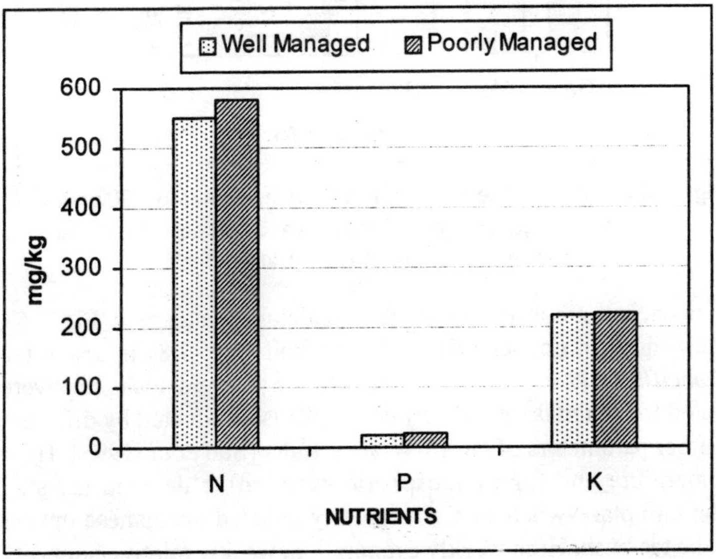

Fig. 3.3: Mean available Nitrogen (N), Phosphorus (P) and Potassium (K) in tea gardens of zone-I of Himachal Pradesh

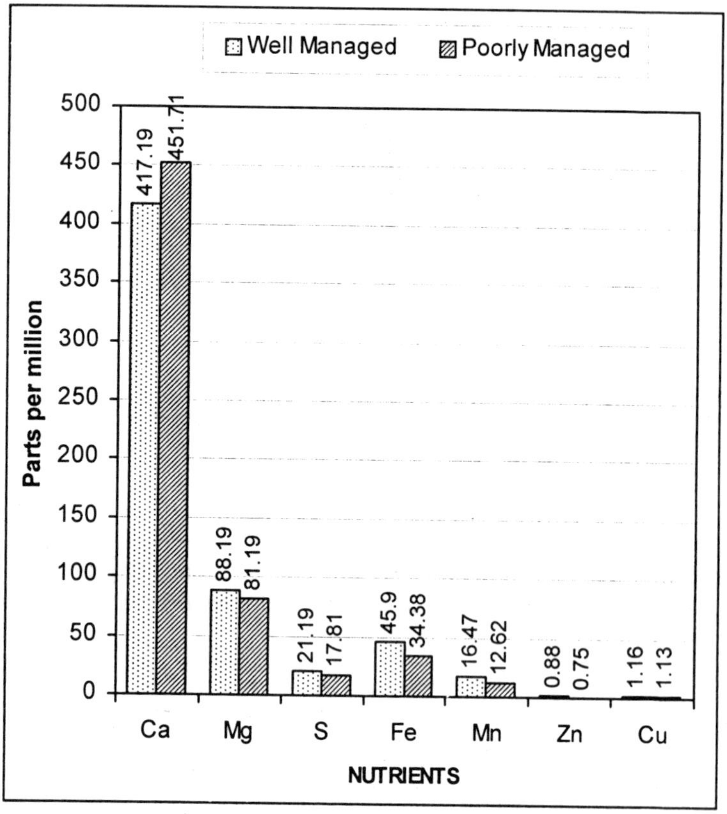

Fig. 3.4: Mean available Calcium (Ca), Magnesium (Mg), Sulphur (S), Iron (Fe), Manganese (Mn), Zinc (Zn) and Copper (Cu) in tea gardens of zone-I of Himachal Pradesh

Concentrations of micronutrients calcium, manganese (Fig. 3.5), zinc (Fig 3.6), copper (Fig. 3.7) and iron (Fig. 3.8) in green tea [*Camellia sinensis* (L) O Kuntze] leaves (Kangra local jat) were related to the uptake capability of tea plants as affected by different weather parameters of North-Western India (Sud *et al.* 1995). High temperature and high atmospheric evaporative demand assisted calcium uptake whereas high humidity reduced manganese uptake by the tea bush. High weekly evaporation, weekly relative humidity and accumulated rainfall were reported to depress the uptake of zinc, copper and iron in green tea shoots.

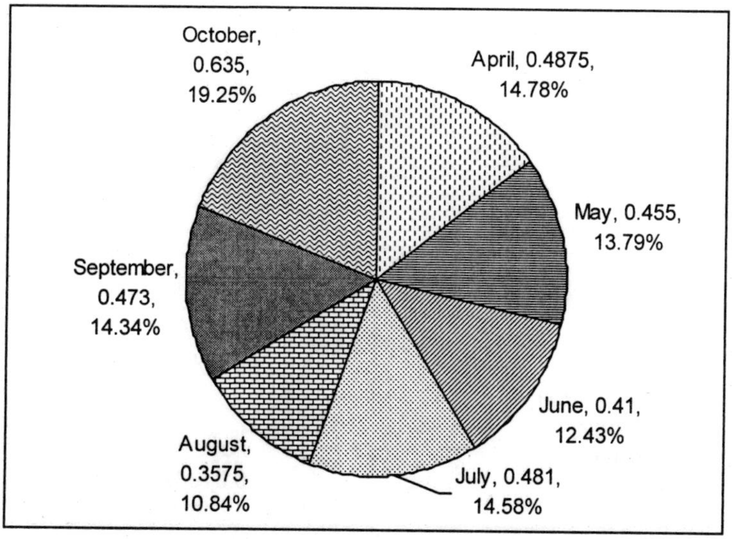

Fig. 3.5: Mean monthly content of Manganese (g/Kg) and its percentage in green tea shoots of Kangra local

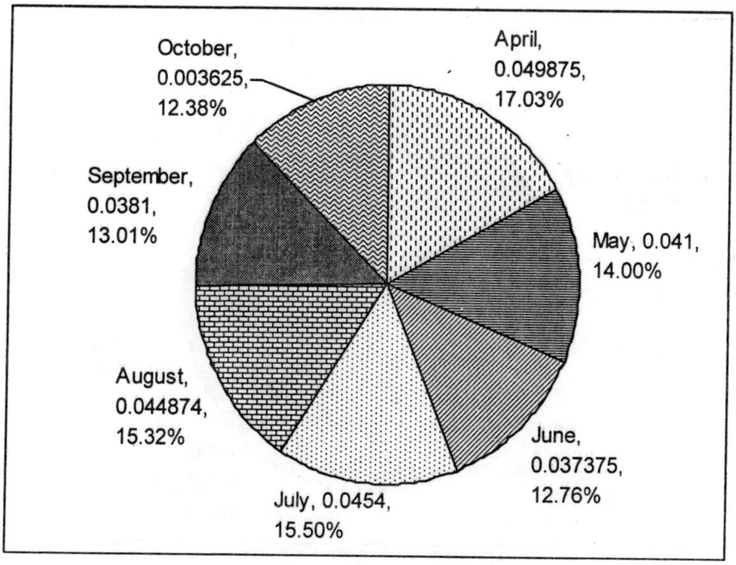

Fig. 3.6: Mean monthly content of Zinc (g/Kg) and its percentage in green tea shoots of Kangra local

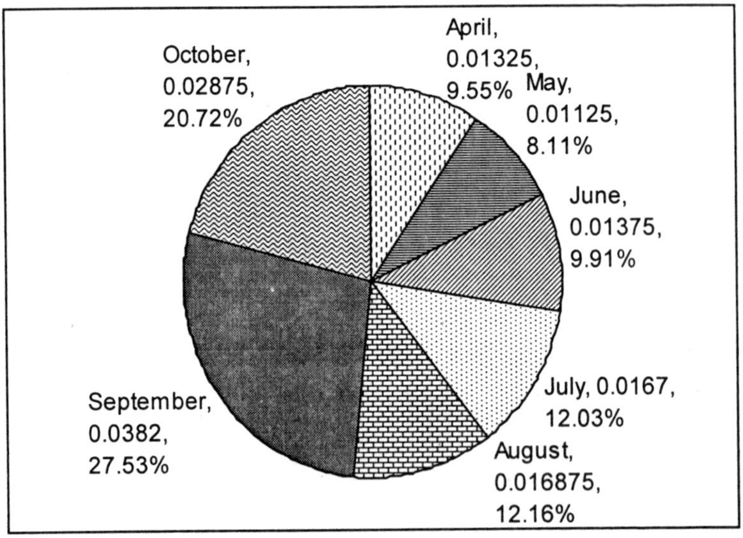

Fig. 3.7: Mean monthly content of copper (g/Kg) and its percentage in green tea shoots of Kangra local

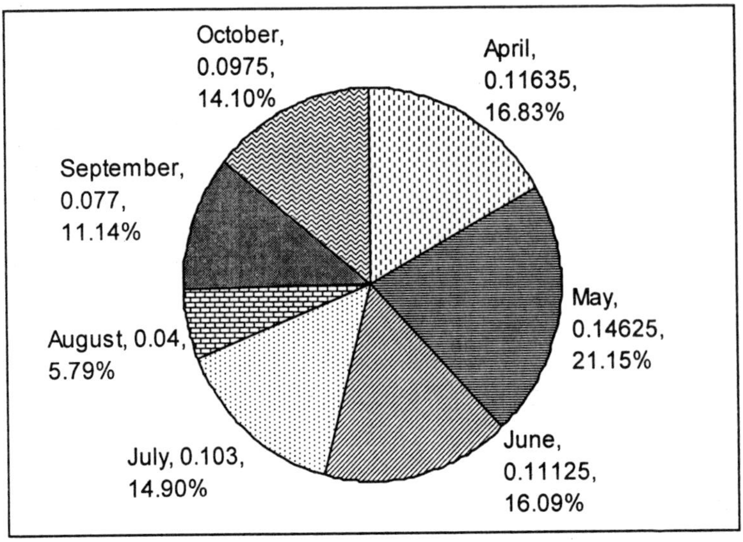

Fig. 3.8: Mean monthly content of iron (g/Kg) and its percentage in green tea shoots of Kangra local

In general, the uptake capability and level of nutrients were determined primarily by ambient temperature, rainfall, relative humidity, growing degree days and evaporation during colder and drier season. However, during the warm season uptake was determined by relative humidity and evaporation. Tea plant uptake capability during an intermediate season was found to be affected by ambient temperature, rainfall and to a lesser degree by relative humidity, evaporation and growing degree days. The solubility of nutrients was a precondition for their availability and uptake by the tea bush. A correlation and regression between nutrient and weather parameters is presented in Table 3.1.

Table 3.1: Correlation and regression between nutrient (calcium, manganese, zinc, copper, iron) and weather parameters (X_1=weekly mean maximum temperature, X_2=weekly mean minimum temperature, X_3=weekly mean temperature, X_4=weekly mean relative humidity, X_5=weekly total mean rainfall, X_6=accumulated seasonal rainfall, X_7=weekly total màn evaporation, X_8=accumulated seasonal evaporation, X_9=weekly mean growing degree days and X_{10}=accumulated growing degree days).

Nutrient Cropping Year	*Regression Equation*	*Correlation Coefficient*
Calcium		
1st	$-0.042 + 0.011X_1 - 0.013X_2 - 0.00008X_6 + 0.0002X_8$	0.680*
2nd	$0.224 - 0.002X_4 + 0.00007X_8$	0.509*
3rd	$0.166 - 0.0004X_5$	0.397*
Pooled	$0.184 - 0.001X_4 - 0.00002X_{10}$	0.197
Manganese		
1st	$1289.6 - 33.48X_2 - 5.66X_4 + 0.257X_{10}$	0.808*
2nd	$1287.6 - 10.742X_4 - 7.547X_7 + 0.343X_8$	0.600*
3rd	$-683.9 - 179.121X_2 + 172.881X_3 + 9.307X_4 + 0.081X_6$	0.710*
Pooled	$1123.2 - 27.408X_2 - 4.367X_4 + 0.45X_8$	0.582*
Zinc		
1st	$60.2 - 0.239X_7 - 0.017X_8$	0.285*
2nd	$55.9 - 0.299X_7$	0.365*
3rd	$33.6 + 1.355X_1 - 1.248X_2 - 0.316X_7$	0.438*
Pooled	$73.4 - 1.13X_1$	0.170

(Contd.)

(*Contd.*)

Nutrient Cropping Year	*Regression Equation*	*Correlation Coefficient*
Copper		
1st	$12.2 + 0.011X_6$	0.640*
2nd	—	—
3rd	$46.7 - 2.676X_2 - 0.019X_6 - 0.331X_{10}$	0.604*
Pooled	$18.3 - 0.023X_6 - 0.126_8 + 0.085X_{10}$	0.399*
Iron		
1st	$173.1 - 1.332X_4$	0.366*
2nd	—	—
3rd	—	—
Pooled	$140.9 - 0.054X_8$	0.116

* Significant at P = 0.05.

It was of interest to note that under identical weather conditions and agro-techniques the pattern of nutrient uptake by different varieties of tea bush was almost similar, however, the amount of uptake varied significantly (Figs. 3.9 to 3.12).

Studies conducted on the varietals and seasonal variations of total-nitrogen, soluble-nitrogen amino acid-nitrogen and polyphenols revealed that the varieties Dhoedham and Khorijan had better quality characteristics followed by Kalline, Runglee and Doom Dooma. The monsoon season affected these chemical constituents adversely and that the quality of early flush season and summer flush season was better than the other seasons (Sud and Badyal 1989). There was hardly any practice to compensate nutrients other than nitrogen, phosphorus and potassium in the tea gardens of Himachal Pradesh. In order to cope with the measures to rectify micro and macro nutrient deficiency in tea gardens of Himachal Pradesh, a systematic study was carried out to analyze green shoots of Kangra local, Chinery hybrid type of tea for potassium, sodium, calcium, phosphorus, magnesium, manganese, iron, copper and zinc (Sud *et al.* 1990). The levels of calcium, magnesium, copper and manganese in tea leaves of Kangra local were found to be lower than desired limit. Although no visual symptoms of deficiency were reported in the foliage, however, it was recommended that the nutrient deficiency be adequately met with in the tea growing regions of Himachal Pradesh if yields are to be increased.

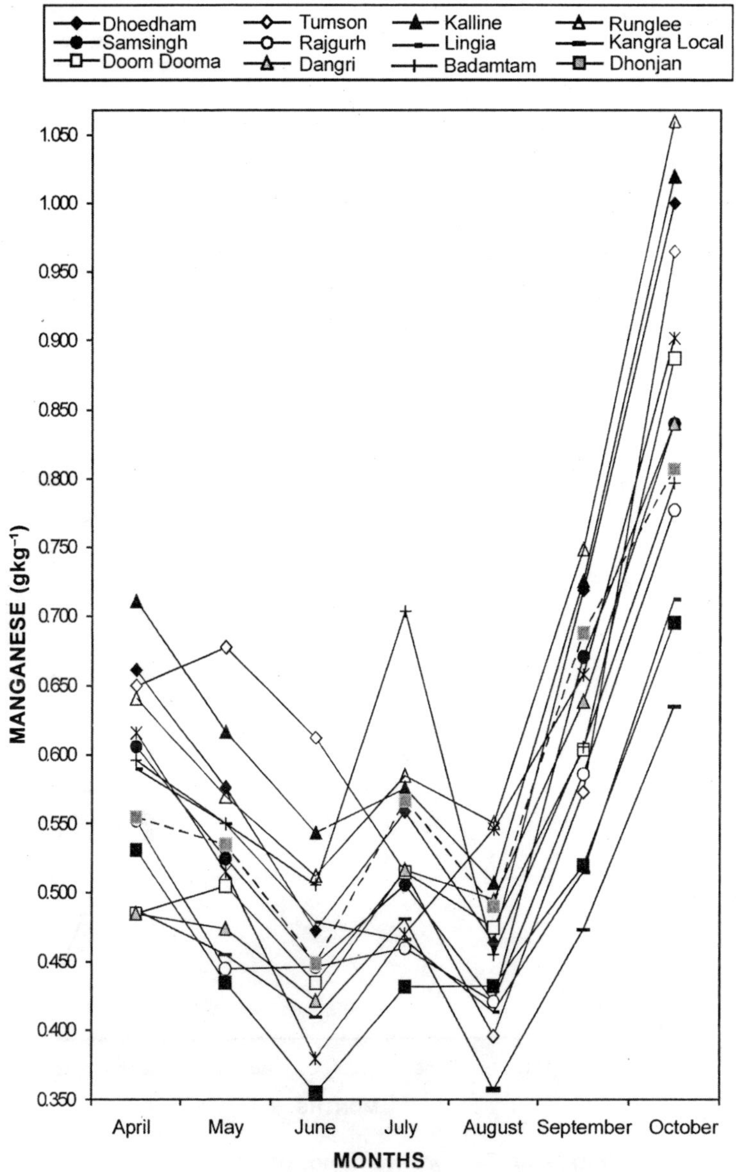

Fig. 3.9: Seasonal variations of manganese in different varieties of tea

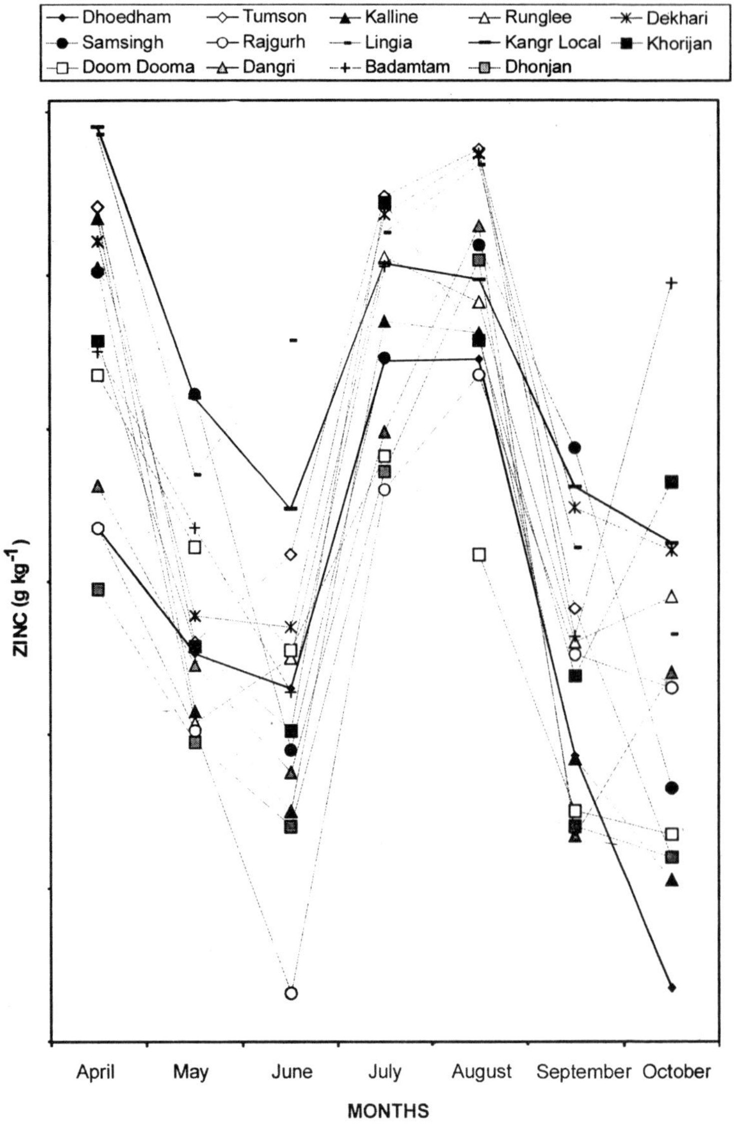

Fig. 3.10: Seasonal variations of Zinc in different varieties of tea

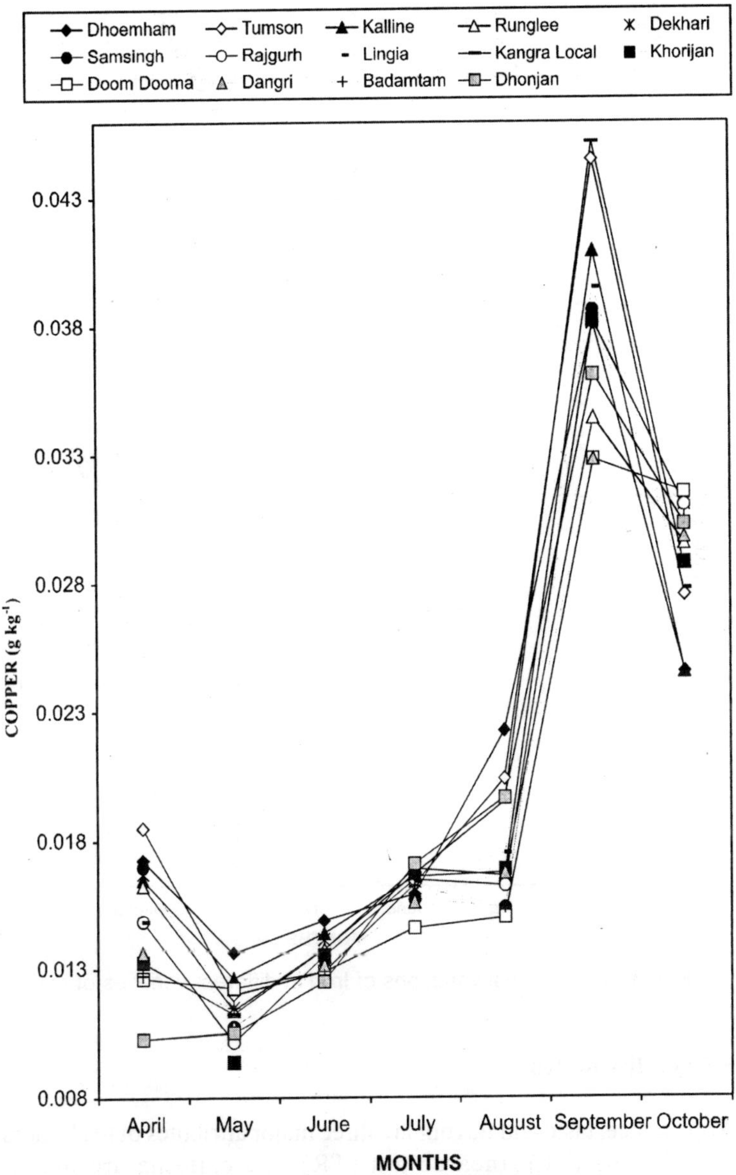

Fig 3.11: Seasonal variations of Copper in different varieties of tea

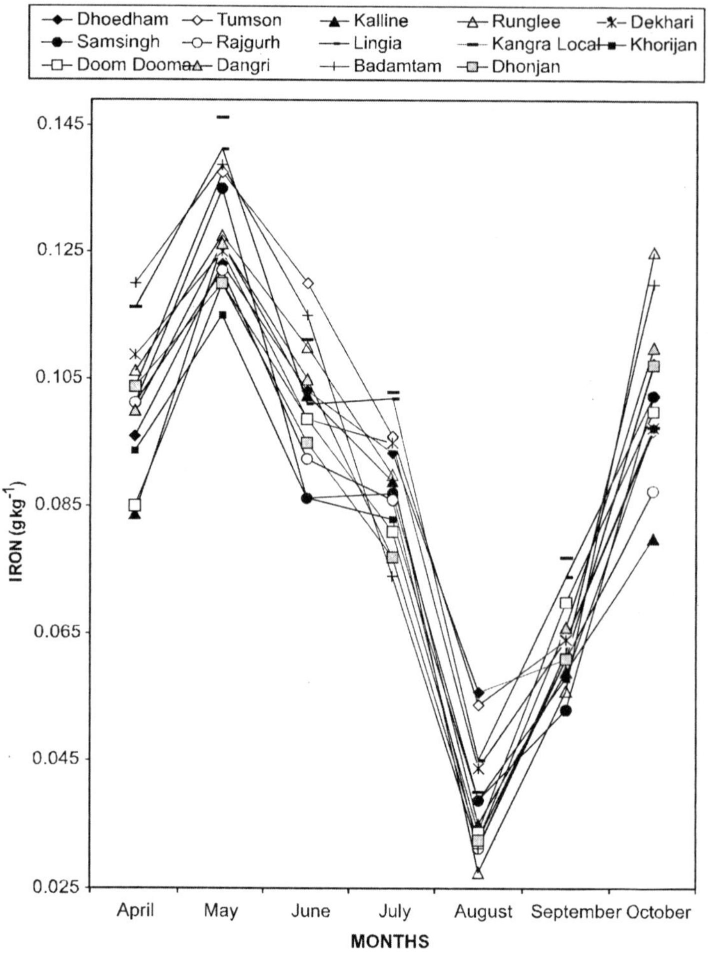

Fig. 3.12: Seasonal variations of Iron in different varieties of tea

3.2 Quality of Tea

Appearance, taste and flavour are three major attributes of tea liquors. Theaflavins (TF), thearubigin (TR) and caffeine are mainly responsible for various infusion characteristics. TF and intermediate weight TR are associated with liquor colour and brightness; caffeine and TF together are responsible for briskness and a very complex mixture of terpenoids and other volatile compounds is responsible for aroma of tea. Agro-climatic conditions, variety of tea, geographical origins/locations and processing technique greatly influence the quality characteristics of made tea. All the above mentioned factors being constant the quality of tea also varies with the flush seasons.

Total nitrogen (N), amino acid N, caffeine and total polyphenols in green tea shoots of 14 seed jats growing at Tea Experiment Station, Department of Tea Husbandry and Technology, CSKHPKV, Palampur, under Palampur agro-climate were estimated throughout four flush seasons (end March-April, May-June, July-August and September-October) during 1986 and 1987 (Sud and Badyal, 1989). The mean values of total N: 4.84 per cent (CD at 5%:0.17), soluble N: 2.43 (CD at 5%:0.19), amino acid N: 1.18 (CD at 5%:0.27), caffeine: 4.07 (CD at 5% 0.32) and total polyphenols: 23.39 (CD at 5%:0.82) were recorded in different varieties of tea. There were significant variations in biochemical constituents between varieties and seasons. Assam type tea clones grown under Palampur conditions had higher levels of estimated constituents. The quality of April and dry season tea was better than the back end crop, however, the quality of tea was adversely affected during the monsoon season.

The commercial orthodox tea from the Palampur Cooperative Tea Factory Limited, Palampur was assessed for polyphenolic oxidation products, liquor characteristics and mineral composition for three consecutive years during 1988 to 1990 (Sud and Bhatacharjee, 1990 and 1992). Total colour and brightness of the tea liquor varied in the range of 0.98-1.11 and 10.31-17.49 per cent, respectively. The thearubigins:theaflavin ratio was reported to be between 10.50 and 12.11 in April tea. The liquor characteristics and hence the quality of early season teas were assessed better than dry season teas. The quality of rainy season teas was the poorest among all the seasons. Tasters' valuations corroborated the observations based on chemical estimations. Withering of 55-60 percent and low difference between the room and floor temperature during fermentation were reported to improve the colour and brightness characteristics of orthodox tea of the main flush-season (July-August) which accounts for about 60 per cent of the total crop. The mineral contents of made tea varied in the range — Copper (Cu): 51-124 µg/g, Manganese (Mn): 534-

763 μg/g, Zinc (Zn): 24-42 μg/g, Iron (Fe): 186-407 μg/g, Calcium (Ca): 0.17-0.36 per cent, Potassium (K): 2.49-2.57 per cent, Magnesium (Mg): 0.18-0.30 per cent and phosphorus (P): 0.22-0.37 per cent.

Similar observations on seasonal variations in infusion quality of orthodox tea were also reported by Gulati and Ravidranath (1996). The TF, TR and caffeine contents were maximum in early-flush tea and declined gradually with progress in season, showed a minimum during main-flush and again improved slightly through backend season. High proportions of provisionally identified flavour constituents: linalool, geraniol, β-ionone, methyl salicylate, phenyl acetaldehyde, trans-2-hexenal and several unidentified compounds were recorded in early flush season and backend orthodox tea of Kangra valley (Fig. 3.13).

Seasonal variations in TF, TR, total colour and brightness (Fig. 3.14) in commercial tea manufactured at the Palampur Cooperative Tea Factory Limited, Palampur were observed for four consecutive years (1993-1996) with a view to evaluate the effects of changing weather conditions on the quality of tea (Sud and Baru, 2000). A degree of 600-650mg/g withering during first, second and fourth season was found optimum for the development of significantly higher brightness and total colour characteristics. The quality of rainy season-flush suffered due to high chlorophyll content and low degree of withering.

However, circulation of hot-air through the withering troughs to assist evaporation of leaf moisture increased the brightness and total colour of rainy season teas.

Withering and brightness exhibited significant negative correlations with high relative humidity and rainfall. The tea liquors of summer season teas were found to be superior in their total colour and brightness characteristics. Correlations among quality parameters, degree of withering and weather parameters of commercial black tea (orthodox) manufactured at the Palampur Cooperative Tea Factory Ltd., Palampur over the years and during different years are presented in Tables 3.2 and 3.3, respectively.

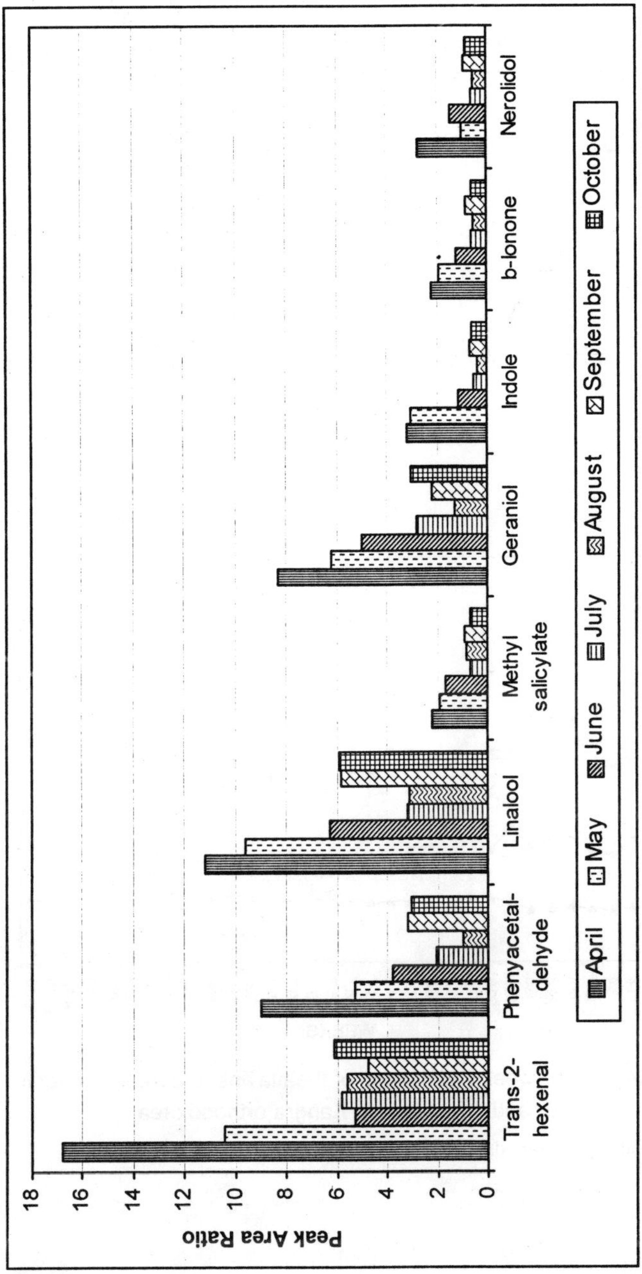

Fig. 3.13: Seasonal variations in aroma components of Kangra orthodox tea

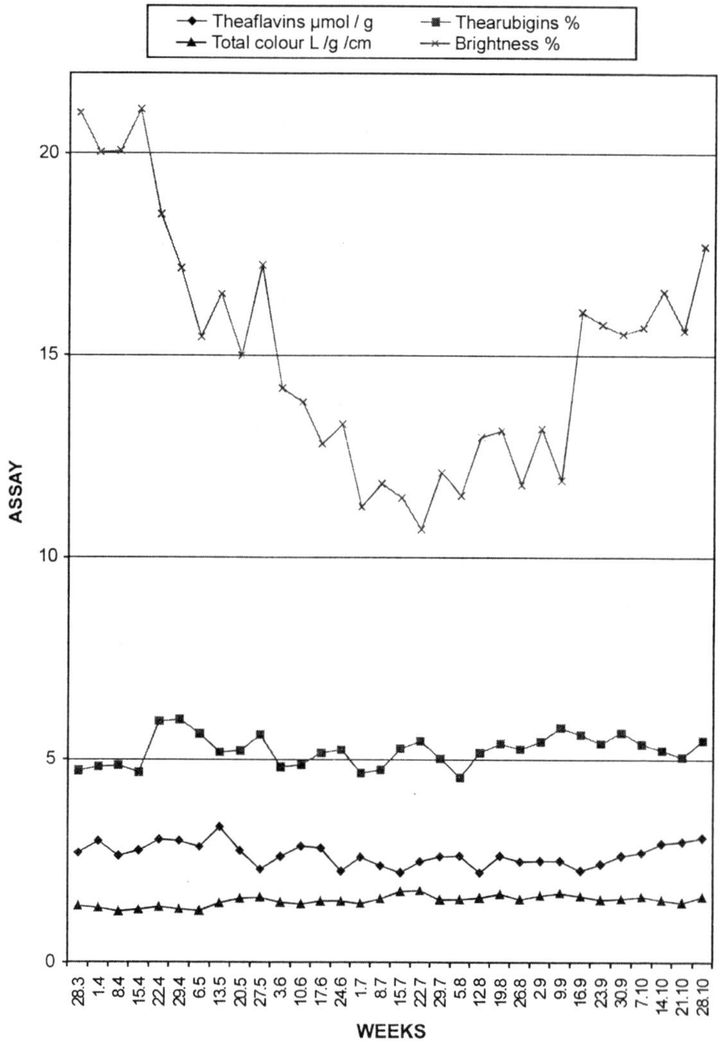

Fig. 3.14: Mean* weekly variations of theaflavins, thearubigins, total colour and brightness in Kangra orthodox tea

*Based upon three years data.

Table 3.2: Correlation among quality parameters of commercial black tea (orthodox) manufactured at the Palampur Cooperative Tea Factory Ltd., Palampur, degree of withering and weather parameters#

Parameter	*Brightness*	*Total colour*	*Withering*	*Theaflavins*	*Min temp*	*Min temp*	*Relative humidity*	*Rainfall*	*Evaporation*
Thearubigins	NS	NS	NS	NS	NS	NS	NS	NS	NS
Brightness		–0.647*	0.784*	0.463*	NS	–0.629*	–0.850*	–0.741*	0.549*
Total colour			–0.715*	–0.520*	NS	NS	0.556*	0.405*	–0.509*
Withering				0.425*	NS	NS	–0.759*	–0.659*	0.692*
Theaflavins					NS	–0.418*	–0.602*	–0.434*	0.401*

* Significant at P = 0.05.

\# Based on three year data.

NS = Non-significant.

Table 3.3: Correlation among quality parameters of commercial black tea (orthodox) manufactured at the Palampur Cooperative Tea Factory Ltd., Palampur, degree of withering and weather parameters during different years (1993-1996)

Parameters	*Year*	*The-aflavins*	*Thearu-bigins*	*Brightness*	*Total colour*	*Withering*
Maximum temperature	1993	NS	NS	NS	NS	NS
	1994	-0.621*	NS	-0.459*	NS	NS
	1995	NS	NS	-0.380*	NS	0.379*
	1996	0.380	NS	NS	NS	NS
Minimum temperature	1993	-0.480*	NS	-0.351*	NS	NS
	1994	-0.726*	NS	-0.766*	NS	-0.601*
	1995	NS	NS	-0.658*	0.351*	NS
	1996	NS	NS	-0.359*	NS	NS
Relative humidity	1993	-0.513*	NS	-0.694*	0.550*	NS
	1994	NS	NS	-0.548*	NS	-0.748*
	1995	NS	NS	-0.380*	0.383*	-0.576*
	1996	NS	NS	-0.632*	NS	-0.732*
Rainfall	1993	-0.394*	NS	-0.365*	NS	NS
	1994	-0.359*	NS	-0.531*	NS	-0.570*
	1995	-0.379*	NS	-0.491*	0.355*	-0.459*
	1996	NS	NS	-0.438*	NS	-0.552*
Evaporation	1993	NS	NS	0.366*	-0.579*	NS
	1994	NS	NS	NS	-0.395*	0.611*
	1995	0.541*	NS	NS	NS	0.619*
	1996	0.622*	NS	0.581*	NS	0.596*
Withering	1993	NS	NS	NS	-0.401*	
	1994	0.351*	NS	0.669*	NS	
	1995	NS	NS	NS	-0.611*	
	1996	NS	NS	0.762*	NS	

* Significant at P = 0.05.

NS = Non-significant.

Table 3.4: Chemical composition of fresh tea shoots

Compounds	*% Dry Weight*	*Contribution*
Total Polyphenols	25 – 30	Astringency
Flavanols		
(+) Catechin	1 – 2	
(–) Epicatechin	1 – 3	
(–) Epicatechin gallate	3 – 6	
(–) Epigallocatechin	3 – 6	
(–) Epigallocatechin gallate	8 – 12	
(+) Gallocatechin	3 – 4	
Flavonols and flavonol glycosides	3 – 4	
Leuco anthocyanins	2 – 3	
Polyphenolic acids and depsides	3 – 4	
Caffeine	3 – 4	Briskness
Theabromine	0.2	
Theaphilline	0.5	
Amino acids	4 – 5	Brothyness
Organic acids	0.5 – 0.6	
Monosaccharide	4 – 5	
Polysaccharides	14 – 22	
Cellulose and hemicelluloses	4 – 7	
Pectin	5 – 6	
Lignin	5 – 6	
Protein	14 – 17	
Lipids	3 – 5	
Chlorophyll and other pigments	0.5 – 0.6	Colour and appearance
Ash (Inorganic – minerals)	5 – 6	
Volatiles	0.01 – 0.02	Aroma

Table 3.5: Biochemical compounds responsible for colour, taste and flavour characteristics of tea

Biochemical compounds	*Characteristics*
Colour	
Theaflavins	Yellowish brown
Thearubigins	Reddish brown
Flavonol glycosides	Light yellow
Pheophorbide	Brownish
Pheophytin	Blackish
Carotene	Yellow

(Contd.)

(Contd.)

Biochemical compounds	*Characteristics*
Taste	
Polyphenols	Astringent
Amino acid	Brothy
Caffeine	Bitter
Theaflavins	Astringent
Thearubigin	Ashy and slight astringent
Flavour	
Linalool, Linalool oxide	Sweet
Geraniol, Phenyl acetaldehyde	Floral
Nerolidol, Benzaldehyde, Methyl salicylate, Phenyl ethanol	Fruity
Trans-2-hexenal, n-hexanal, cis-3-hexanol	Grassy
B-Ionone	Fresness

3.4 Tea Diseases

Blister Blight

The most destructive diesese of tea [*Camellia sinensis* (L) O Kuntze], occurs under cool humid climate in almost all tea growing areas. The existence of blister blight is known since 1868 in upper Assam which subsequently spread to Darjeeling and other parts of tea growing area. All the tea leaves and stems are not susceptible to the attack of *Exobasidium vexans*; the older tissues are less susceptible to its infection.

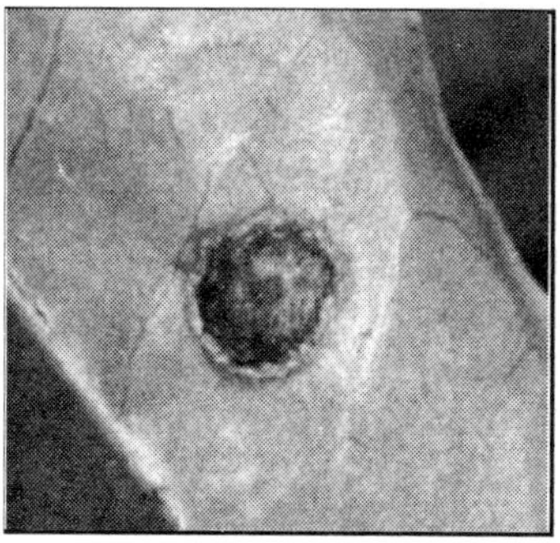

Early Symptoms or Blister Blight

Developed Blister Blight

The symptoms first appear on young expanding leaves as pale yellow or pinkish translucent spots which gradually enlarge to a circular lesion. As the lesion develops further the upper side of the leaf is depressed into a shallow cavity and the lower side becomes convex forming the typical blister. The upper concave surface of the lesion is smooth and shiny, while the lower convex surface is dull at first, turns gray and finally becomes powdery as it sporulates.

The affected leaves often become folded or irregularly rolled up owing to the development of lesions. Under severe infection, the affected leaves curl up and become distorted. The wind-borne spores get lodged on the surface of a suitable host tissue and germinate under favourable conditions and cause fresh infection. The disease is caused by *Exobasidium vexans* Massee, a basidiomycetous fungus (Exobasidiales, Exobasidiaceae) with no known alternate or collateral host.

Its occurrence in Himachal Pradesh tea gardens was first recorded by Saharn and Chouhan in 1968-69 (Saharan and Chouhan 1972); it remained a minor disease until 1985. The disease appeared in an epidemic form in most of the tea plantations during the monsoon season of 1986, resulting in 10-20 per cent loss in yield. *Exobasidium vexans*, the causal agent of blister blight of tea was reported to survive on necrotic blisters during off-season (Sugha 1997). The foci of infection were reported to be the volunteer seedlings growing under the mother bushes where the disease first appeared during second or third week of March every year for its major outbreaks during September and October under Palampur conditions (Fig. 3.15).

Correlation with weather variables indicated that the disease had a significant positive correlation with the minimum and average temperatures and relative humidity; however, significant negative correlation was reported with average rainfall and sunshine hours. December-pruned tea bushes were reported to be less infected compared to the tea bushes which were pruned in the month of June the period for the production of new succulent growth and the climate favourable for the disease. Avoidances of pruning of tea bushes during the month of June and shade were recommended for alleviating the ravages of blister blight under Himachal Pradesh conditions (Sugha *et al.* 1990). On the basis of study conducted to evaluate the efficacy of fungicides against blister blight of tea Blitox + nickel chloride,

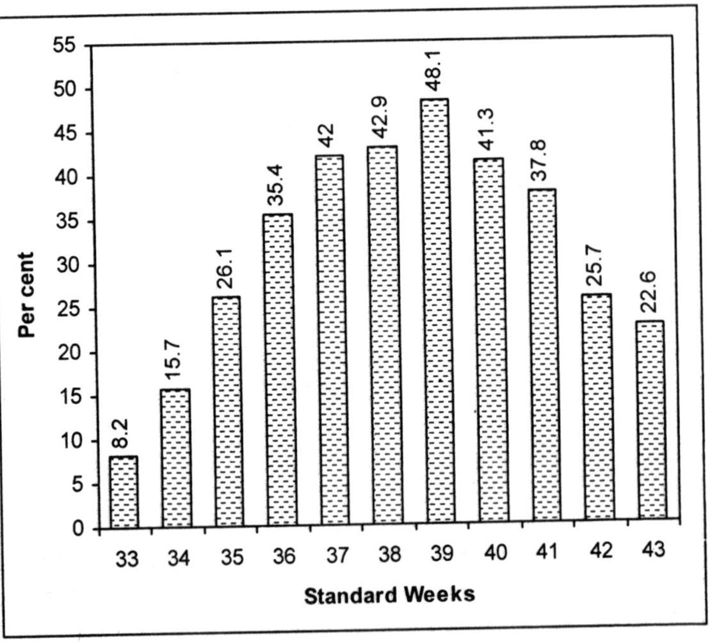

Fig. 3.15: Incidence of blister blight of tea observed in Himachal Pradesh

Calixin or Baycor were reported to be more effective in controlling blister blight of tea (Sugha and Singh 1990). Baycore and Systhane were evaluated effective during prolonged wet periods.

Blister blight disease adversely affects the quality of made tea. The extent of quality deterioration of orthodox tea of Himachal Pradesh was reported by Sugha *et al.* (1991) (Fig. 3.16). Gulati *et al.* (1993) also reported marked changes in the total polyphenol, catechins, total nitrogen, amino acids, chlorophylls and polyphenol oxidase activity in tea shoots (Fig. 3.17). Liquor characteristics vis-à-vis colour, brightness, briskness, theaflavins, thearubigins and caffeine in orthodox tea made from infected shoots exhibited progressive decline with increasing disease severity (Fig 3.18). The magnitude of aroma components vis-à-vis hexane-1-ol, phenyl acetaldehyde, linalool, methyl salicylate, geraniol, indole, β-ionone, nerolidol in Himachal Pradesh tea was also reported to decline with disease intensity (Fig. 3.19).

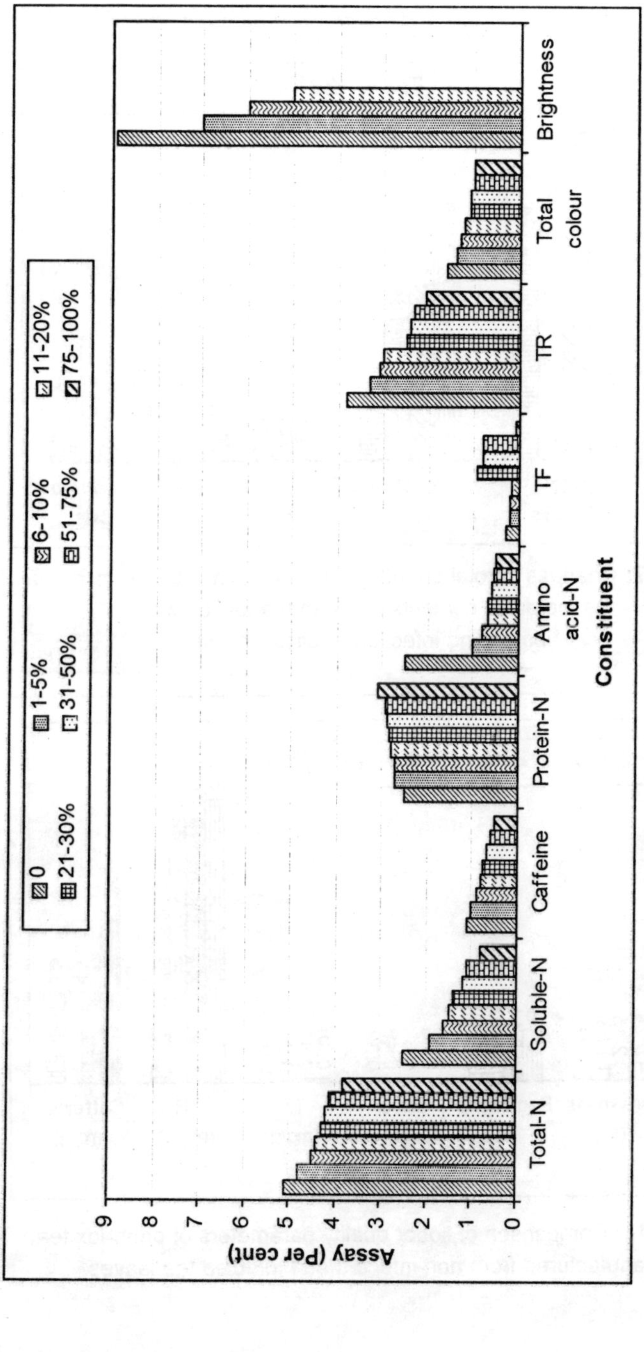

Fig. 3.16: Effects of blister blight severity on the chemical constituents of orthodox tea

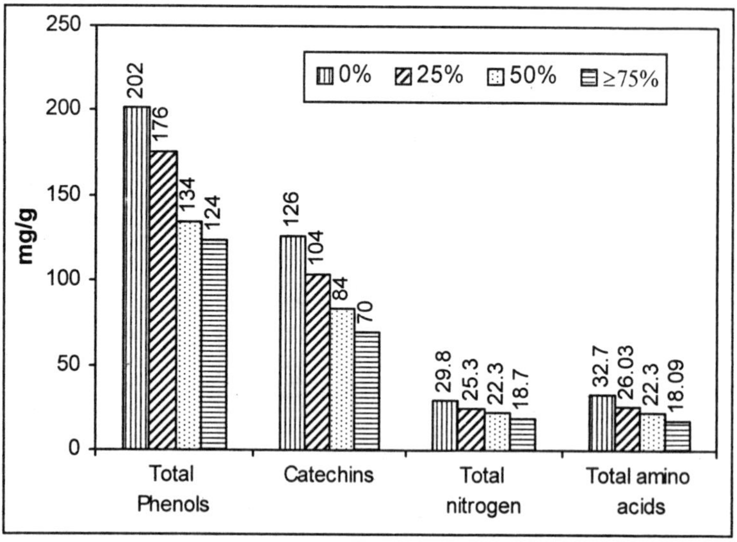

Fig. 3.17: Changes in total phenol, catechins, total nitrogen and total amino acids contents in green tea leaves with increasing infection of blister blight

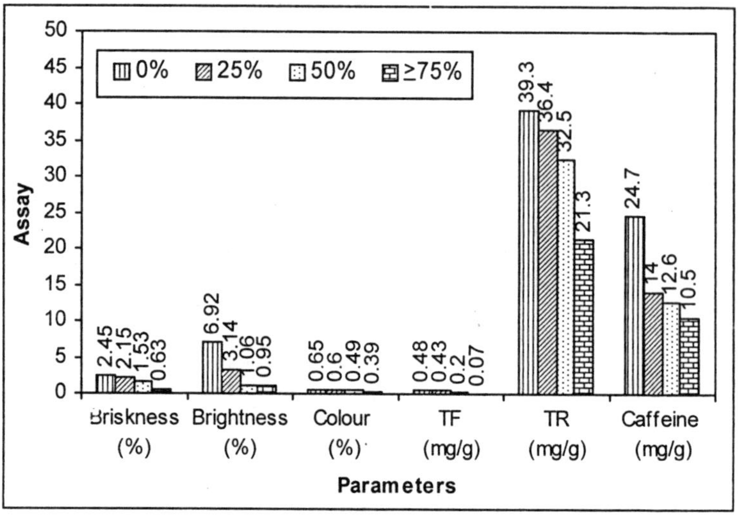

Fig. 3.18: Comparison of liquor quality parameters of orthodox tea manufactured from non-infected and infected tea leaves

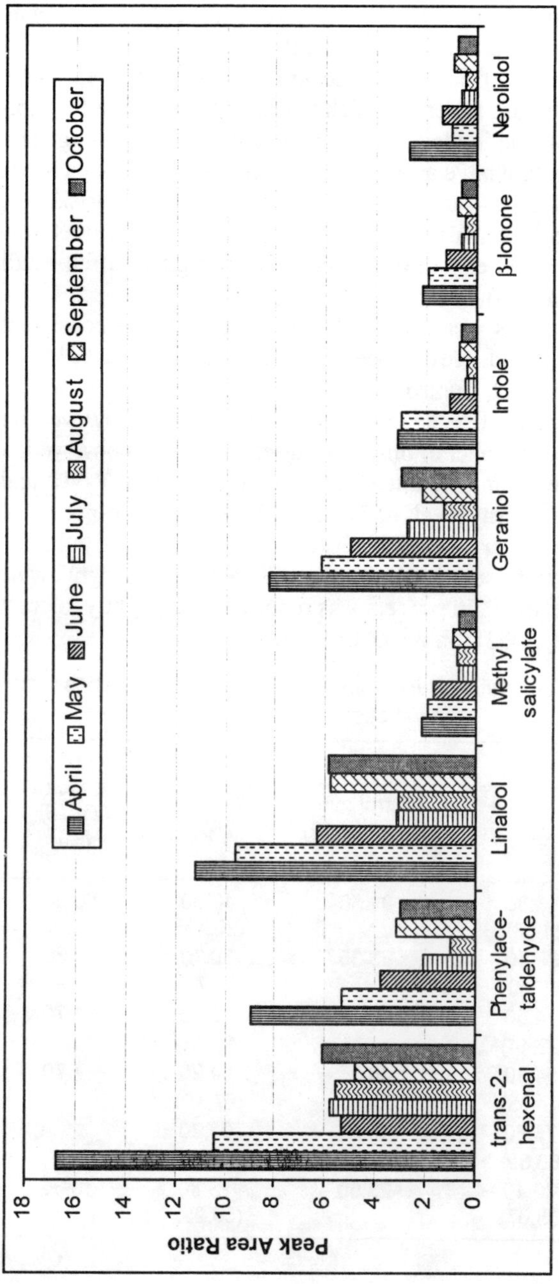

Fig 3.19: Monthly variations in aroma constituents in tea due to increasing intensity of blister blight

Reduction in flavour of tea made from infected shoots was attributed to decrease in levels or total loss of linalool, phenyl acetaldehyde, geraniol, β-ionone and several unidentified components with increasing disease severity which was also responsible for non-uniform withering and inadequate rolling during tea processing. The fungal infection might have affected various flavour precursors in tea shoots. The decline in various infusion characteristics (briskness, brightness and colour) in tea processed from infected shoots was attributed to lower contents of theaflavins, thearubigins, caffeine and high-polymerized substances.

Gamma radiations were reported to cause significant consistent increase in per cent incidence of blister blight disease and diseased leaves in Kangra local, Lingia, Tumsong and TV 18 cultivars over seedlings raised from unirradiated seeds (Sugha and Paul, 1996). However, no significant effect on number of blister per diseased leaf was observed.

Of the nine recommended tea cultivars two cultivars, P-312 and Kangra Asha with severity levels of 7.60 and 12.30 per cent, respectively, were reported to be tolerant against blister blight compared to cultivars TV-8 and TV-18 with severity level of 91.20 per cent. Kangra Jwala with severity level of 30.70 per cent was reported to be slightly tolerant (Thakur and Paul, 2002) (Table 3.6).

Table 3.6: Varietal tolerance/susceptibility of tea genotypes against blister blight

Vrietay	*Exobasidium vexans*			*Control over check (TV 18) (%)*
	Incidence %	*Control over check* (TV 18) *(%)*	*Severity* %	
Kangra Asha	16.80 (24.18)*	81.50	12.30 (20.43)	86.50
Kangra Jwala	33.40 (35.20)	63.30	30.70 (33.71)	66.30
P 312	14.60 (22.44)	84.00	7.60 (15.94)	91.70
TV 1	54.10 (47.33)	40.60	84.20 (67.45)	7.70
TV 8	75.60 (60.69)	16.90	91.20 (73.69)	
TV 9	70.40 (55.07)	22.60	73.30 (59.25)	19.60

(Contd.)

(*Contd.*)

Vrietay	Exobasidium vexans			Control over check (TV 18) (%)
	Incidence %	Control over check (TV 18) (%)	Severity %	
TV 23	73.30 (58.96)	19.50	73.40 (59.62)	19.50
TV 253	45.30 (42.31)	50.20	56.80 (48.98)	37.70
TV 18	91.00 (72.80)		91.20 (73.38)	
CD (0.05)	(5.40)		8.24	

* Figures in parentheses are angular transformed values.

3.5 Tissue Culture

The importance of tissue and organ culture for rapid mass multiplication and improvement of plants is well recognized. Mass propagation of selected tea clones using cotyledonary explants was attempted by Sood *et al.* (1993). The Institute of Himalayan Bioresource Technology (IHBT), Council of Scientific and Industrial Research (CSIR), Palampur laboratories appeared to be the first to obtain viable synthetic seeds of *Camellia sinensis* of Himachal Pradesh. Four types of responses (*i*) direct shoot formation, (*ii*) somatic embryogenesis, (*iii*) callus induction and proliferation and (*iv*) direct root formation were supported by electronic microscopy, histological and cytological studies. The impact of thidiazuron [N-phenyl-N-1,2,3,-thiadizol-5 ylurea] (TDZ) and benzylaminopurine (BAP) on the micropropagation of *Camellia sinensis* var China hybrid using nodal segments from *in vitro* raised seedlings was evaluated (Mondal *et al.* 1998). Extremely low concentrations of TDZ (1pM-100nM) compared to higher concentrations of BAP (1-10μM) were reported to be effective in inducing shoot bud proliferation and maintaining high rates of shoot multiplication on hormone-free media. The explants treated with TDZ were reported to yield healthy shoots, with sturdy leaves even during initial stages of growth. However, the initiation of shoot buds in medium containing BAP in combination with auxins required continuous presence of plant growth regulators to sustain proliferation rates.

Low concentrations to commensurate with its high cost and high proliferation rates; TDZ was evaluated to be potent cytokinin for tea micropropagation. The protocols on tea micropropagation of Sood *et al.* (1993) were further improved by Sandal *et al.* (2001) who reported TDZ (2.5 to 5.0μM) to promote tea shoot proliferation with healthy shoot growth in 20 mL static liquid medium [Basal medium: MS (Murashige and Skoog 1962) medium supplemented with 3 per cent sucrose with or without 0.8 per cent agar] with subculture period at an interval of six to eight weeks. 80 per cent plant survival after 60 days in jars containing sand and soil mixture and 60 per cent survival in pots under green house condition after 120 days was reported.

Tea microshoots excised from well established multiple shoot cultures grown *in vitro* and 8-week-old three- to five-leaved seedlings from a local chinery stock and UPASI-9 (from South India) were selected as scions and rootstocks, respectively for auto and heterograft (Fig. 3.20). Grafts on four month old seedling-raised rootstock during early summer were reported to have performed better in terms of establishment and per cent survival of plants transferred to the field (Prakash *et al.* 1999).

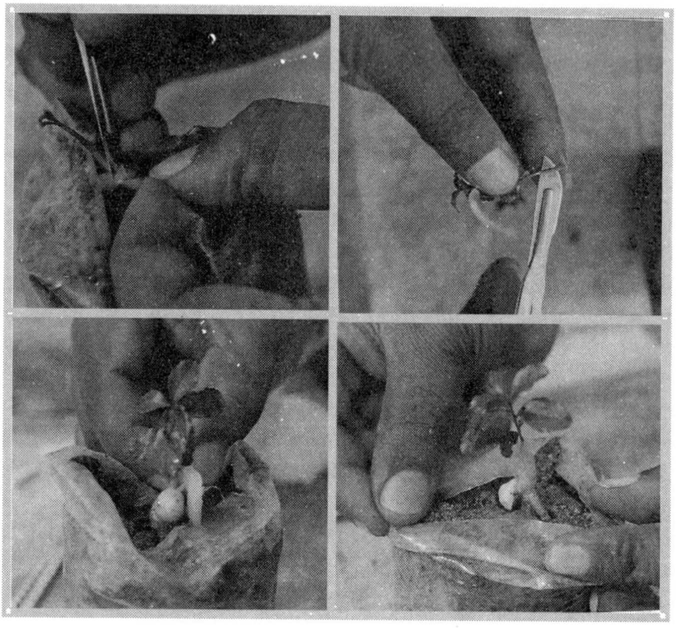

Fig. 3.20: Grafting in Tea

No significant difference was observed between auto- and hetero-grafting. Propagation by single node cutting and varietal improvement by conventional breeding technique being slow; micropropagation techniques that take relatively short time for introducing improved clones, however, suffered from loss due to lack of hardening and thus establishment in the field. Significant success for hardening was repoted by Sharma *et al.* (1999) when the microshoots of 3-4 cm size having short internodes harvested during spring and early summer seasons, treated with 500 mg L^{-1} IBA for 30 minutes and raised in specially designed hadening chamber with CO_2 (9.09/10 × 10^{-5} mol L^{-1} to 10.22/10 × 10^{-5} mol L^{-1} and 20/11 × 10^{-5} mol L^{-1} to 80/13 × 10^{-5} mol L^{-1}) enrichment, light (15 μ mol m^{-2} s^{-1}) and in soil of pH 4-6.4 (Fig. 3.21).

Fig. 3.21: *a.* Microshoots; *b.* Rooted Microshoots; *c.* Specially Designed Hardening chamber; *d.* Hardened Plants in Pots

Variety, stage in terms of explant collection for maximum somatic embryogenic response from tea seeds was reported by Mondal *et al.* (2000). Kangra jat was found to be superior than genotypes TG 270/2/B, UPASI-9 of *Camellia assamica* (Masters) (Assam type) and T-78. The germination efficiency of cold storage embryos was reported to decline as compared to untreated embryos. The germinated embryos were hardened and transplanted to the field successfully. A premier protocol for the production of transgenic tea [Camellia sinensis (L) O Kuntze cv. Kangra jat] via Agrobacterium-mediated genetic transformation of somatic embryos with a view to serve as an experimental basis for desirable gene introgression aiming at the genetic improvement of tea was developed and reported (Mondal *et al.* 2001).

Induction of *in vivo* embryogenesis was reported to be regulated by temperature-dependent gene present in tea. In three cultivars namely UPASI-9, T-78 and Kangra jat studied, the embryogenesis was reported to occur at 28°C in all. Histological studies corroborated the findings (Mondal *et al.* 2001a). A consistently high frequency of tea somatic embryos was obtained by following a protocol for efficient induction, growth and development and germination.

Protocol:

(*i*) Primary embryo induction medium: Half strength of MS medium supplemented by NAA (2.0 mg/L) and BAP (2.0 mg/L).

(*ii*) Secondary embryo formation medium: MS medium modified with 10.31 mmol/L ammonium nitrate, 9.39 mmol/L potassium nitrate and 1.5 m mol/L potassium sulphate.

(*iii*) Embryo development medium: Further supplementation of the above (*ii*) with BAP (2.0 mg/L), IBA (0.2 mg/L) and glutamine (1.0 mg/L).

(*iv*) Embryo germination medium: Removal of potassium sulphate from the above medium

An achievement of up to 52 per cent germination of the ambryos was reported by removing potassium sulphate from the medium in step *iv*.

Tea somatic embryos' normal development or germination could not be evoked by treatments like chilling and gibberellic acid (GA_3). The poor and abnormal germination of tea was reported to be due to non-storage of carbohydrate reserves by the embryos during maturation phase and external agents failed to bring about their mobilization. However, improvement of conversion frequency was reported when carbohydrates reserves were supplemented from external sources like sucrose and maltose; readily available forms of carbohydrates (Mondal *et al.* 2002). These observations corroborated earlier findings regarding tea somatic embryos incapability to accumulate carbohydrates in the form of storage reserves.

Attempts were made to develop a system for the production of artificial seeds in tea employing viable propagules like axillary buds, and effect of low-temperature storage on bud sprouting efficiency with a view to explore the possibilities of effective storage of axillary buds for transportation and exchange of germplasm of tea (Mondal *et al.* 2002a)

Storage of artificial seeds of tea at 4°C was reported to reduce sprouting period in axillary buds by 15 days without affecting the viability of micropropagation. The process of seed development of tea [*Camellia sinensis* (L) O Kuntze] was studied in order to identify the maturity index and time of seed collection (Bhattacharya et *al.* 2002). In tea plants about 18 months period, from flower-bud initiation to mature seed development was observed. Initiation of buds was recorded during mid- to late-May in peak flowering season with subsequent enlargement into white buds with a differentiated calyx during June. About 85 per cent of the flowers opened during July-August when insect-mediated cross-pollination was reported to result into fertilization followed by zygote formation in 50 per cent of the ovaries and fruit initiation/setting was reported to occur during September-October. The fruit growth and seed development was studied for one complete year after fruit setting to mature tea seed yield. The maximum rate of seed dry matter accumulation was reported to coincide with the accumulation of starch in the embryos during maturation phase when the embryo abscisic acid (ABA) content was also highest. However, the level of endogenous free embryonic ABA which was high was reported to decline during embryo maturation phase which in turn was reported to be associated with a rapid decline in total sugar content. Mature tea seeds with 30.6 per cent moisture content were found capable of germination, however, on one month storage the tea seeds moisture content declined to 19.3 per cent which resulted in to decline in germination percentage to 59.8. The studies confirmed the inability of tea seeds to tolerate desiccation. In order to understand developmental aspects of tea seeds, as affected by changes in major types of plant growth regulators, the role of endogenous auxins (indole-3-acetic acid, IAA) was investigated (Bhattacharya *et al.* 2004). The state of continuum even at full maturity and lack of clear end point to seed development as indicated by the persistence of appreciable proteins content in all the seed parts confirmed the recalcitrant nature of the tea seeds. The total RNA at high moisture content was reported to decline with progressive decline in moisture content.

A study was conducted by Sharma *et al.* (2003) to have an insight into the role of ABA with respect to abnormal maturation, poor germination frequency of somatic embryos and desiccation tolerance of tea seeds. The results corroborated the hypothesis regarding inability to accumulate the requisite amount of storage reserves to be the cause for abnormal and precocious germination of somatic embryos of tea, put forward by Mondal *et al.* (2002). Higher ratios of starch to TSS in the ABA treated embryos as compared to control did reflect the conversion of simple sugars into complex polysaccharides and hence higher storage reserves in the maturation stage of somatic embryos. Increase in total protein content and appearance of high molecular proteins in the embryos in response to desiccation stress were reported. The role of ABA in inducing proper maturation through the expression of certain middle range proteins in the desiccated embryos treated with ABA was investigated to understand the probable mechanism of desiccation tolerance in relation of ABA (Sharma *et al.* 2004).

3.6 Tea Breeding

In order to make selections from tea (*Camellia sinensis*) clones for breeding through hybridization Paul *et al.* (1994) reported TV23 to be the highest yielder followed by P-312, TV9 and Tukdah 253 compared with Kangra local. The quality of TV 23 and Tukdah 253 was excellent in terms of theaflavin content and brightness of made tea samples. Theaflavin exhibited positive significant genotypic correlation with total colour and per cent brightness. Total colour also showed positive significant genotypic correlation with per cent brightness and thearubigins. Of the 200 tea bushes selected on phenotypic basis at Chambi tea estate during 1992; only 10 bushes which had most of the desirable characteristics were finally selected for breeding purpose. Among the introduced cultivars, TV 23 was specifically adapted to favourable environments with highest yield potential, whereas T 253 had the general adaptability (Paul *et al.* 1995). The radio-biological effects of gamma-rays were investigated. On the basis of LD_{50} values, the genotype TV 18 (*Camellia assamica*) was reported to be more radio-sensitive than Lingia, Tumsong and Kangra local (*Camellia sinensis*) with respect to primary branches, secondary branches, internodal length and survival percentage; whereas opposite trend was observed with respect to leaves per plant and plant height (Table 3.7). However, among *Camellia sinensis,* Lingia was reported to be relatively more radio-resistant (Paul *et al.* 1996).

Table 3.7: LD_{50} values of tea cultivars for different growth parameters

Growth Parameter	*Gamma-rays (kR)*			
	C. assamica		*C. sinensis*	
	TV 18	*Lingia*	*Tumsong*	*Kangra Local*
Primary Branches	4.38	7.50	6.96	7.85
Secondary Branches	0.44	8.26	1.00	0.78
Leaves per plant	8.86	9.59	5.97	7.41
Internodal Length	5.31	11.60	5.67	6.95
Plant Height (cm)	13.45	6.55	5.50	5.05
Survival (%)	3.01	4.65	4.19	3.80

Studies on 13 indigenous lines along with three checks viz., Nanda Devi, Kangra Jwala and Kangra Asha were carried out during 1997 and significant genetic variability was reported among the selections for all the traits studied. In general, high heritability coupled with high genetic advance was also observed for all the traits studied. On the basis of high yield and good quality two genotype viz. B_{57} and B_{61} were identified for future breeding programme (Dogra and Paul 1997). Besides high yield, high density of plucking points was reported to be another important constituent of an ideal tea plant which in turn can be obtained by increasing secondary branches, surface area of the bush and length of growing shoots (Dogra &Paul 2002).

On the basis of three parameters, productivity (x_i), responsiveness (bi) and stability (S^2 di), it was reported that TV 23 was adapted to favourable environment with highest yield potential, T 253 had the general adaptability whereas Kangra local adapted to poor environment with the lowest yield (Tabie 3.8).

Table 3.8: Estimates of adaptability parameters for yield with respect to different cultivars

Cultivars	x_i	*bi*	S^2 *di*
Kangra Local	383.70	0.43*	5.50**
P 312	867.60	1.23*	26.00
T 253	856.20	1.17	7.90**
TV9	847.60	1.06	14.60**
TV18	651.20	0.85	19.60**
TV 23	1007.10	1.25*	18.10**
General mean	768.90		
SE:t	39.50	0.10	

* Significantly different from unity at 5 per cent level
** Significantly different from zero at 5 per cent level

Due consideration for the presence of g x e interaction was recommended for the identification of a tea cultivar for a particular locality (Paul and Gupta 1996).

Amplified Fragment Length Polymorphism (AFLP) markers were successfully employed to detect diversity and genetic differentiation among Indian and Kenyan populations of tea (Paul *et al.* 1997).Shannon's index of diversity was used to partition the total phenotypic variation into, between and within population components. On average, most of the diversity was detected within populations, with 79 per cent of the variation being within and 21 per cent being between populations of Indian and Kenyan tea (Table 3.9).

Table 3.9: Partitioning of the diversity into within and between populations of Indian and Kenyan tea for five primer combinations

Primer Combination	H_{sp}	H_{pop}	H_{pop}/H_s	$(H_{sp} - H_{pop})/H_{sp}$
1. E33/M39 (E_{aag} M_{aga})	3.30	2.61	0.79	0.21
2. E34/M39 (E_{aat} M_{aga})	3.46	2.77	0.80	0.20
3. E37/M32 (E_{acg} M_{aac})	3.46	2.77	0.80	0.20
4. E42/M39 (E_{agt} M_{aga})	3.46	2.77	0.80	0.20
5. E46/M32 (E_{att} M_{aac})	3.53	2.73	0.77	0.23
	X3.44	2.73	0.79	0.21

E_{aag} $M_{aga,}$ $E_{aat,}$ E_{acg} $M_{aac,}$ $E_{agt,}$ E_{att} M_{aac} = priemer basis; H_{sp}=diversity within population H_{pop}=diversity of whole population

A dendrogram constructed on the basis of band sharing distinctly separated the three populations of tea into China type (*sinensis*),

Assam type (*assamica*) and Cambod type (assamica *ssp. lasiocalyx*) in a manner consistent with the present taxonomy of tea. The principal coordinate (PCO) plot clearly demarcated the Assam, China and Cambod types. The China type accessions from different areas in a tea estate were reported to form sub-groups within the China type group showing clear geographical sub-differentiation. Kangra Asha and Kangra Jwala the selections from the Tea Experimental Station, Palampur were reported to differ extensively for AFLPs (similarity = 0.55). Kangra Jwala was reported to resemble Assam type and Kangra Asha was considered one of the original China type varieties. It was also reported that the Indian and Kenyan teas have common ancestor.

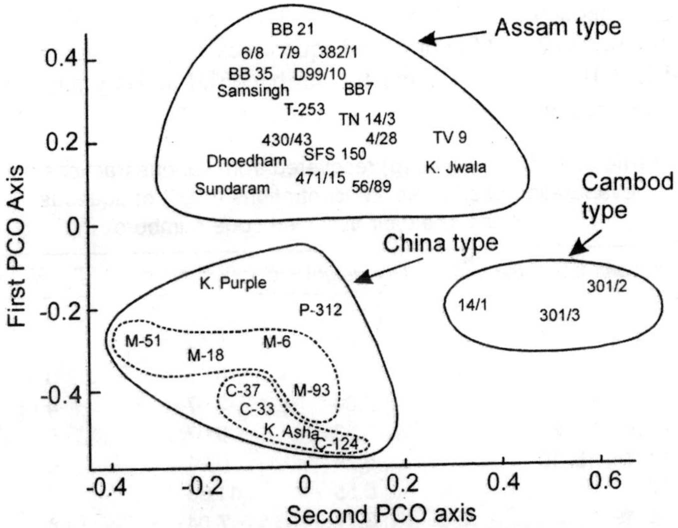

Fig 3.22: Principal coordinate plot of 32 genotypes of tea (*Camellia sinensis*). Two principal components accounted for 32.56 per cent of the total variation

3.7 Antibactrial Activity

Although references on seasonal variations of theaflavins, thearubugins, quality characteristics and mineral composition are available in literature (Sud and Bhattacharjee 1992, Sud *et al.* 1995, Gulati and Ravindranath 1996, Sud and Baru 2000), there is hardly any information regarding health related benefits and antibacterial activity of the tea of Himachal Pradesh. Multifunctional activities of green and black teas have been reported to be due to the presence of catechins, a group of polyphenolic compounds in tea. However, most studies on the health benefits of tea have been focused on green teas rich in unoxidised flavanols or the tea catechins: epicatechin, epigallocatechin, epicatechin gallate and epigallocatechin gallate. A study was carried out to investigate antibacterial activity of Himachal Pradesh tea against some selected bacteria (Sud *et al.* 2005 communicated).

Methanolic extract of made black tea was fractioned using an activated silica gel column. A solvent system with increasing polarity was used (Ethyl acetate, Ethyl acetate: methanol:: 80:20, Ethyl acetate:methanol::50:50, Methanol). Twelve aqueous solutions of the fractions/pooled fractions and aqueous extract of fresh tea shoots (Table 3.10) were evaluated for antibacterial activity against 11 selected bacteria.

Table 3.10: Dry weights (g) recovered from various fractions on evaporation of solvents, concentrations (g L^{-1}) of aqueous solutions and their assigned code numbers

Fraction/Pooled fraction	*Dry weight*	*Concentration*	*Assigned code*
1	20.81	37.62	1
2, 3, 4	1.62	2.64	2
5, 6, 7	0.51	0.65	3
8	2.00	2.97	4
9, 10, 11, 12	3.23	6.07	5
13, 14, 15, 16	0.24	0.21	6
17	6.55	11.65	7
18, 19	3.71	7.04	8
20, 21	1.62	0.35	9
22	1.05	0.18	10
23, 24, 25	0.90	0.18	11
26, 27	0.20	0.40	12
Caffeine	—	1.43	13
Aqueous fresh tea shoot extract	Not detected		14

The aqueous extracts of fresh tea shoots and that of the first fraction eluted with ethyl acetate were potent and their inhibitory effects were highest when compared with the fractions/pooled fractions eluted later (Fig. 3.23). The antibacterial activity decreased with the order of elution; the fractions eluted last and caffeine did not exhibit antibacterial activity. *Serratia marcescens*, *Shigella dysenterae* and *Escherichia coli* (local isolate) were totally resistant to all the extracts.

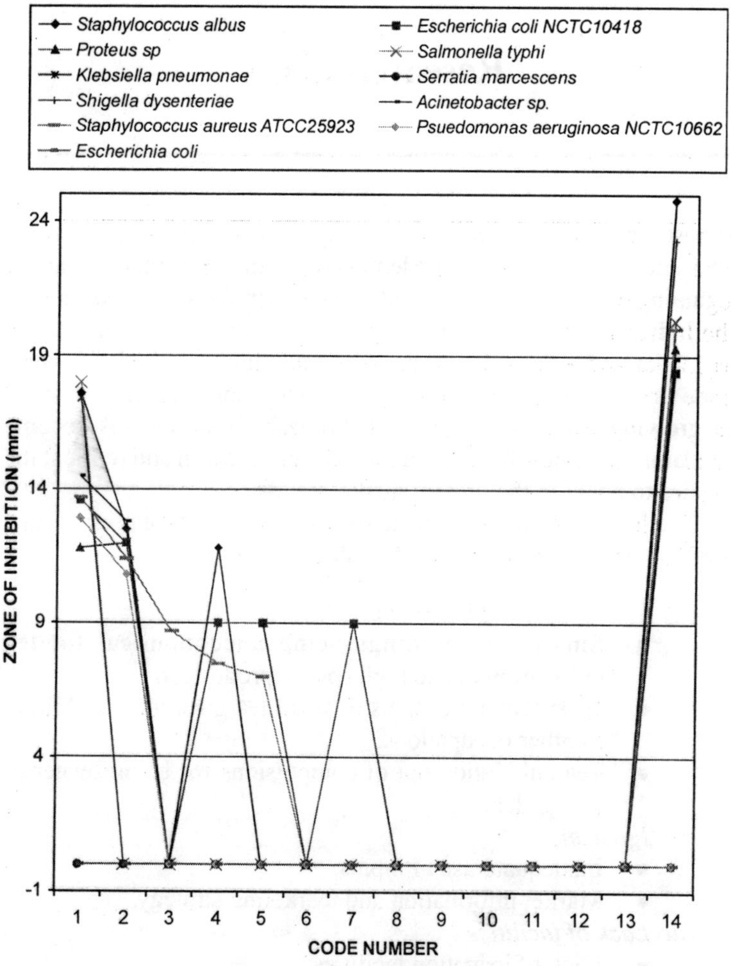

Fig 3.23: Antibacterial activity of methanolic extract of orthodox tea of Himachal Pradesh

4

Research Gaps

Almost three times increase in the production was recorded between 1985 and 1998; however, sudden decrease in tea production at the beginning of 21st Century is a matter of concern for State Government. The Indian tea market is witnessing a stiff competition from China, Sri Lanka and Kenya due to the new trade initiatives of the World Trade Organization. The competition is all the more stringent for small tea growing States like Himachal Pradesh. Hence it has become mandatory to review the gaps in the existing research and reorient the policies to adapt to the present market trends.

The following factors seem to be responsible for the present state of affairs of the tea of Himachal Pradesh:

(*i*) *Lack of interest in tea cultivation*
- Small land holdings being uneconomical for tea cultivation due to high cost of production.
- Poor economic status of small tea growers and shifting to other occupations.
- Tea cultivation out of compulsions for being owner of tea garden.

(*ii*) *Ignorance*
- Inadequate use of inputs.
- Market information and marketing strategy.

(*iii*) *Lack of facilities*
- Lack of irrigation facilities.
- Lack of new planting materials.
- Lack of information about value addition.
- Lack of technical advancement of tea factories.
- Unavailability of labour during peak season.

(*iv*) *Cost factor*

- High cost of inputs.
- High labour cost.
- Unavailability of primary wholesale market in Himachal Pradesh.

(*v*) *Other factors*

- Age of tea bushes.
- Lack of skilled operators for various tea operations.
- Lack of national and international markets for direct export.
- Low quality of major flush (rainy season) tea.
- Absence of brand name and logo of Kangra tea.
- Lack of consumer awareness drives.
- Lack of domestic consumption.
- Lack of advertisement campaign.
- Lack of timely availability of various inputs.

The mandates of organizations involved in research and extension activities are not clearly defined. The recommendations sometimes differ; for example the recommendations on fertilizer dose especially that of potassium is not in unison. No extensive work on the nutrient deficiency symptoms and diseases, except blister blight seems to have been carried out. There is hardly any reference of studies on the economics of tea production, marketing and price realization. There are no endeavours to formulate and popularize tea based products. Likewise there has been no opinion poll survey conducted to assess consumers' predilection for this tea; in and outside the state. Lack of awareness among the consumers about the unique characteristics of Kangra tea seems to have affected its popularity. Popular brand name and logo of Kangra tea specifying the qualities associated with its origin need to be highlighted if the tea of Himachal Pradesh is to take off.

Tea cultivation system has undergone various changes from time to time. Heavy doses of fertilizers and other agrochemicals were applied to attain higher productivity. These practices though increased yield, made the plant system more vulnerable to various stresses like infestation of pests, besides deleterious effect on the environment. The effects of synthetic chemicals and the associated environmental degradations have led to the emergence of 'back to nature' movement, the concept of traditional farming also known as 'organic farming'.

Owing to the fact that toxic chemical residues accommodate in human beings through the food chain, consumers prefer to buy organically-grown food items. It is, therefore, reasonable to surmise that with the onset of trade liberalization, the Himachal Tea Industry is also on the threshold of a new global competition and there is an urgent need to focus on emerging trends.

To attract a larger clientele there is a strong need to improve quality and go for value addition. Containing the cost of production will benefit the people engaged in tea industry.

5

Identification of Areas of Short-term and Long-term Research

Tea has gained more importance than any other commodity (as a consequence of multilateral trade agreements of the World Trade Organization) due to its export potential. Despite the agreeable climate and soil conditions the tea industry in Himachal Pradesh has not flourished up to the expectations. The Government of India and the tea producing States have started taking initiatives to meet the challenges. It is, therefore, imperative to review the policies and set the priorities.

Exhaustive data bank on various aspects of tea to gaze into the crystal ball of tea industry of Himachal Pradesh is readily available. Recently the Kangra tea has acquired the Geographical Indications status and hence it calls for an independent existence in the world tea market.

Although Himachal Pradesh is not a major tea producing state, however, the tea of Himachal Pradesh has distinct quality and flavour attributes that put it into its own class. It is, therefore, imperative that new approaches are worked out for the future of Himachal Pradesh tea.

5.1 Suggested Thrust Areas

- Mother Bush selection.
- Physiological evaluation of clones for specific traits.
- Documentation and cataloguing of germplasm.

- Refinement of vermin-culture technology and application of vermin-composting.
- Nutrient management on stomatal behaviour and growth of young tea plants.
- Comparative soil plant nutrient status with respect to organic and inorganic agriculture.
- Intercropping in tea plantations.
- Improvement of tea quality through blending.
- Efficacy of bio fungicides against tea diseases.
- Product diversification.
- Value addition.
- Developing technology to curtail the cost of production.

6

Policy Implications

6.1 Tea Board India

The Tea Board India is a statutory organization established under the Tea Act, 1953 by the Government of India. Controlled by the Ministry of Commerce and Industry, the Board comprises an executive Chairman and 30 non-official members representing the tea industry, labour and trade as well as common interests. The Board carries out its mandate laid down in the Tea Act, Rules and various Control Orders issued by the Central Government from time to time.

Tea Board India since its inception has been engaged in promoting, conducting and evaluating tea research in India in order to provide effective scientific inputs regarding yield enhancement, quality tea processing, development of value added products and allied fields in tea trade etc. It has its own center, Darjeeling Tea Research Center at Kurseong that looks after the area specific technical aspects of hill tea gardens. Major financial support is extended to Tea Research Association (TRA) in the North East and United Planters' Association of South India (UPASI) in South India which have elaborate research facilities with field experimental stations, research departments and advisory services. Tea Board also supports National Tea Research Foundation (NTRF) an organization that undertakes and promotes, by extending financial support to various research institutes and universities. Research on specialized topics of basic and applied aspects of tea not covered by all the traditional research is also provided support. Tea Board also monitors and coordinates with the research organizations, tea trade and government bodies to provide technical support to the tea trade. The Apex body maintains close coordination with the tea trade and provides feedback to the research institutes and vise versa (Figs. 6.1 and 6.2).

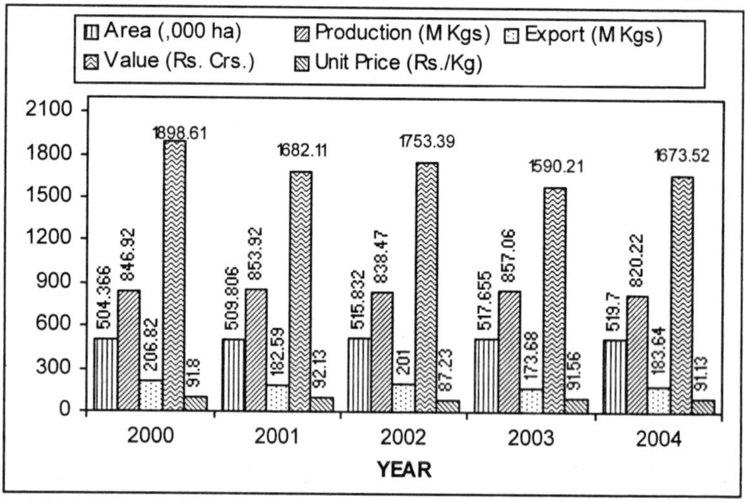

Fig. 6.1: Area under tea, production, export, total value and unit price of Indian tea during 2000 to 2004*

* *Estimated data source*: Facts of Indian Tea, www.indiateaportal.com

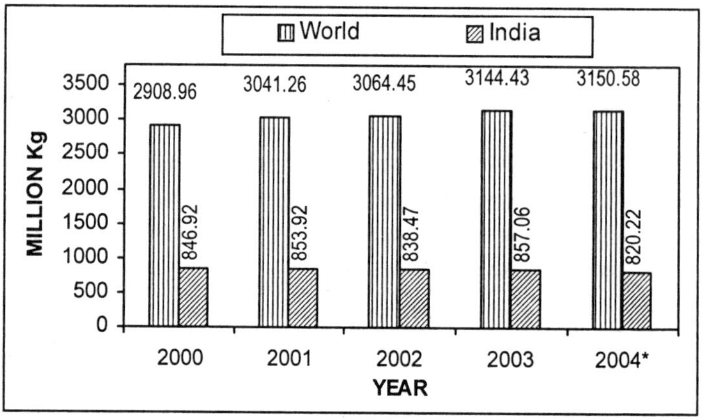

Fig. 6.2: Comparison of world and Indian production of tea (2000 to 2004*)

* *Estimate source:* Tea Board of India Monthly Report of Tea for the month of October, 2005.

6.1.1 Functions of the Tea Board

(*i*) *Development*: Improving yields of tea gardens and upgradation of quality through modernization of tea factories and extension services to growers.

(*ii*) *Promotion*: Popularizing Indian teas and the consumption of this beverage, both at internal and foreign markets.

(*iii*) *Regulation*: Implementing various statutory provisions for the control of the tea industry and trade.

(*iv*) *Statistics*: Collecting data and disseminating information on tea periodically to various stakeholders for effective policy intervention and initiatives.

(*v*) *Labour Welfare*: Supplementing the efforts of various agencies involved in welfare activities among tea garden workers through project specific grants and financial assistance schemes.

(*vi*) *Research & Development*: Grants to institutions for carrying out research in tea science and technology and development projects.

6.1.2 Major Steps Taken By the Government to Help the Tea Industry

(*i*) Considering the financial difficulties faced by the tea Industry, the Indian Bankers' Association (IBA) was persuaded to extend a special relief package to the industry. Accordingly, IBA had issued guidelines to all its member banks in February 2004 to extend a Special Tea Term Loan (STTL) for the tea sector. The package provides for restructuring/rephasing of irregular portion of outstanding term/working capital loans of the tea companies with repayment over 5 to 7 years and a moratorium of 1 year. The STTL also provides for working capital up to Rs. 2 lakhs at a rate not exceeding 9 per cent to small growers.

(*ii*) A sum of Rs. 23.25 crore was allocated to Tea Board for implementing an ad hoc price subsidy scheme for small tea growers for a four month period from February to May 2004. Through this scheme, subsidy was extended to small growers at the rate of Rs. 2 per kg of green leaf harvested by them during the same period.

(*iii*) A price sharing formula between small tea growers and manufacturers of tea at an approximate 60:40 ratio is being implemented w.e.f. 1.4.2004 with a view to ensure that the small growers get a reasonable share of the price for the green leaf supplied by them to the manufacturers. As per this formula, the manufacturers are required to provide 60 per cent of the net sale proceeds to the small growers as long as the price fetched by them for the made tea remains either at par or below the state average. When the sale price of the tea exceeds the state average, the differential between the sale price and the State average needs to be shared between the grower and the manufacturer in the ratio of 50:50.

(*iv*) The import duty on items of machinery used to improve productivity and quality of tea, including value addition, has been reduced to an all inclusive rate of 5 percent.

(*v*) An Inter-Ministerial Committee, set up by the Ministry of Labour, has also studied the issues relating to the plantation sector, particularly the social costs, provident fund dues of the plantation workers and taxation structures. The recommendations of this Committee are under consideration of the Government.

(*vi*) In order to address the various problems of the industry and draw up a long term strategy for sustained growth of tea sector, a stakeholders' conference on challenges before Indian tea industry was organized jointly by the Ministry of Commerce and Industry and Tea Board in New Delhi on 16th and 17th September, 2004. The conference was attended by the representatives of all the sections of the tea industry including producers, workers, labour unions, traders, researchers, State Governments, concerned Ministries of Government of India etc. A whole range of issues on tea relating to production, productivity, research, reforms, marketing, taxation and legislation covering land and labour laws etc. were discussed. In all, twenty five recommendations emerged at the end of the conference. A Tea Advisory Committee comprising 31 members representing all the important segments of the industry has been constituted to oversee the implementation of the recommendations.

It is expected that overall improvement in productivity, cost reduction, a conscious effort towards improvement of quality and better management practices would go a long way in reviving the tea industry and ensuring welfare of the workers.

6.1.3 Schemes

Various schemes have been formulated by the department of Commerce, Government of India and implemented through Tea Board for tea growers in general and small tea growers in particular to facilitate tea plantations, tea processing and packaging etc. The Price Stabilization Fund Scheme (PSFC) was launched in April, 2003 with a view to provide sustained, long-term support to the small growers of tea, coffee, rubber and tobacco. The scheme envisages participation between the growers and the Government and provides financial assistance to enrolled growers in the event of price decline below a specified level. Some of the major schemes are appended in Tables 6.1 and 6.2.

Table 6.1: Scale of assistance under plantation development schemes of Tea Board

Nature of Scheme	*Activity*	*Unit Cost Per Hectare (Rs.)*	*% to Unit Cost*	*Enhanced Rate Per Hectare (Rs.)*
Subsidy	Replanting, Replacement Planting (Plain gardens)	2,10,000	25	52,000
	Replanting, Replacement Planting (Hill gardens)	2,50,000	25	62,000
	Replanting, Replacement Planting (Darjeeling Hills)	2,77,000	25	69,000
	Rejuvenation-Pruning and Infilling	64,000	25	16,000
	Rejuvenation-Pruning and Infilling plus interplanting	88,000	25	22,000
	New planting in SG sector in non-traditional areas of NE States including Sikkim and Uttranchal	2,77,000	25	69,000
	New planting by small tea growers in traditional area (Plain gardens)	1,52,000	25	38,000
	New planting by small tea growers in traditional area (Hill gardens)	2,00,000	25	50,000
	Irrigation	*Capital cost	25	New

* Subsidy for irrigation is extended @ 25 per cent of capital cost or Rs. 10,000.00 per hectare, whichever is less, towards irrigation equipments and creation of irrigation sources such as check dams, tube wells etc.

When the loan and subsidy is considered for Replantation/ Replacement planting, total assistance shall be limited to 80 per cent of unit cost. The unit cost includes planting and maintenance upto 5th year. Hill cost is applicable for Tellah areas of Cachar and Tripura.

Table 6.2: Name, nature of assistance and rate of assistance of various schemes

Name of the Scheme	*Nature of Assistance /Nature of Activity*	*Rate of Assistance*
Small Growers Development	Subsidy/Supply of inputs at subsidized costs for planting of tea	Rs.28,000.00 per hectare
New Area Development	Subsidy/Tea plantation in non-traditional areas of Himachal Pradesh	Rs.40,000.00 per hectare
Plantation Development	Loan/(A) Extension Planting – Replanting and Replacement planting	Rs.1,28,000.00 per hectare
	Loan/(B) Irrigation Equipments	Rs.50,000.00 per garden
	Subsidy/Replanting — Replacement planting	Rs.40,000.00 per hectare
	Subsidy/Rejuvenation — pruning and infilling	Rs.13,000.00 per hectare
	Subsidy/Rejuvenation pruning and infilling with interplanting	Rs.17,000.00 per hectare
Tea Processing and Packaging Development	Loan / (A) Replacement of work out machineries for the processing in existing factories	Rs.50,000.00
	(B) Creation of packaging facilities	
	Loan/(C) Generation of power, transport vehicles and leaf carrying vehicle	50% cost of plant and machinery
	(D) Setting up of Cooperative tea factories	

With time there is not only need to modernize factories but take up new technologies developed in the recent years in the fields of automation, electronics and use energy saving devices. Since there is always good demand for quality tea; modernization and technology upgradation assumes added significance. Accordingly a scheme has been formulated to provide financial assistance to the needy tea gardens/factories with a view to facilitate the tea gardens/factories towards production of good quality of teas suiting eminently to the tastes and preference of the consumers in order to fetch remunerative returns for the tea sold.

- The processing of tea in tea factories should be geared up by replacement of old and worn out machinery and equipment.
- Replacement of machinery has to be a regular exercise depending upon the working condition of the machineries.

At present only 35 to 40 per cent of tea is sold in package form and the rest in the form of loose tea. During the 10th plan period major thrust is on more value realization through:

- Improving the packaging standards.
- Increasing the volume of value added teas.
- Increasing the volume of specialty teas such as green teas, flavoured teas, ready to drink teas etc.
- Product diversification.
- Incentives to the tea factories and packaging units opting for participation in certification programmes.

Tea Board proposes to extend financial assistance by way of subsidy @ 25 per cent of the actual cost.

Under the Rejuvenation and infilling subsidy scheme an amount to Rs.13,36,843.00 benefiting 97 tea growers of Himachal Pradesh was provided for an area of 97.05 hectare from March 2001 to April, 2005. During the year 2004 an amount of Rs. 2,40,000.00 was also provided for upgradation of a tea processing unit in Himachal Pradesh.

6.1.4 Expert Committee

The Tea Board approved the formation of an Expert Committee consisting of Professor N.K. Jain, Scientist Emeritus, Dr. I.D. Singh, Head, Botany, Tea Research Association, Toklai, Assam, Dr. N. Satyanarayana, Head, Botany, Tea Research Institute, UPASI and Mr. Vijay Dudeja, Chairman and Managing Director, Paramount Tea Marketing Private Limited, Kolkota for the evaluation of tea development activities in Kangra with positive recommendations for future developments. This committee undertook a study of Kangra tea plantations with the following objectives:

- Studying the role of all the agencies associated with the development of Kangra tea industry;
- Functioning of Cooperative Factories/Marketing Society/ Planters' Association;
- Assess the survey results for identifying nontraditional tea areas;
- Find out the maladies affecting the tea industry and
- Suggest the ways and means of amelioration in order to attain the desired levels of production and quality.

The expert committee visited different places and conducted an exhaustive study from 15.4.1996 to 19.4.1996 and finalized its report on 22.4.1996. On the basis of assessment of activities carried out by different institutions and agencies involved in the development of tea a Strength-Weakness-Opportunity-Threat (SWOT) analysis was presented (Table 6.3).

The Expert Committee also identified following types of constraints being faced by the tea in its development:

Of the Agencies Involved in Development of Tea

- Inadequate funds (except the TOT).
- Man-power requirements were inconsistent with the diverse functions.

Policy Constraints

- Medium and long-term development policy not well defined.
- Policy in respect of shade management, felling of trees, cleaning of private jungles inconsistent with the needs to enhance productivity.
- Land acquisition restrictions put a stop to expansion of area and induction of professional managers by preventing entrepreneurs.

Operational Constraints

- Lack of effective coordination.
- Duplication of research and recommendations.
- Lack of professional tea makers.
- Lack of irrigation facilities.

Table 6.3: SWOT Analysis

Institutions/ Agencies	*Strength*	*Weakness*	*Opportunity*	*Threat*
Council of Scientific & Industrial Research (CSIR), Palampur (Presently Institute of Himalayan Bioresouce Technology (IHBT)	i. Infrastructure ii. Qualified personnel for research iii. A good track record in transfer of technology leading to high credibility iv. Facilities for tissue culture	Emphasis on basic research Inadequate experienced personnel for transfer of technology in near future Lack of finances for transfer of technology	Leadership in transfer of technology Collaboration with the HPKV for applied research to develop package of practices Standardization of MRL's for pesticides	Likely loss of personnel trained in the transfer of technology in immediate future
Himachal Pradesh Krishi Vishvavid-yalaya	Long term trial plots	Infrastructure for the transfer of technology does not exist No teaching programme for UG/PG course and training to the farmers Lack of focus on tea amongst the other crops handled	Collaborative applied and fundamental research jointly with CSIR for the development of package of practices	Role limited to publication of research papers for promotion as a measure of their programme
Industries Department, Technical Officer Tea (TOT)	Availability of large amount of fund Routing input subsidy through Kangra Marketing Society Availability of infrastructures for raising 2 lakh nursery plants	Sizeable amount of resources spent on establishment Poor choice of planting material in nursery raising Lack of hardening facility in the nursery Poor demonstration plots with too many units supervised by few technically trained personnel	Committee does not envisage any effective future role	Same as opportunity

(Contd.)

(*Contd.*)

Institutions/ Agencies	*Strength*	*Weakness*	*Opportunity*	*Threat*
Tea Board	Access to Central Government funds and resources Coordination through funding of above agencies involved in tea research and development	Lack of trained technical personnel for technical monitoring advice and supervision of development programmes	To play a core effective role in policy planning and implementation of programmes of tea development, supply of inputs and shade regulations	Frequent transfer of staff may adversey affect development programme
Tea Federation	NCDC support	No defined role Not economically viable at present	Can play a nodal role Can coordinate the acivities of cooperative factories Value addition	Lack of economic viability Allocation of factory Conflict of interest with other agencies Accumulated losses Non-business like operation Poor member loyalty
Cooperative Factories	Government suppot and leasing Better equipment than small growers factory Exposure in Calcutta auction	Bottleneck in capacity utilization Low capacity utilization due to lack of leaf supply Have to accept far quality leaf Interference from non-professionals One factory has no tea maker, another employer one only recently High cost of production Accumulated losses	Expanding market & flavouring teas Darjeeling crops stagnation Potential for quality improvement Room for cost reduction	
Marketing Society	Nearness to producing areas leading to better interaction Good member loyalty Sound financial position	Non-professional auction operation Marketing secondary goods	Promotion of Kangra green tea for higher returns	Lack of marketing professionals Lack of infrastructure

Infrastructural Constraints

- Withering and sorting operations delayed during peak season.
- Insufficient space at the disposal of the Cooperative Marketing Society, Amritsar.
- Low labour efficiency.

The Expert Committee stressed the need for paradigm shift from subsidies to incentives; from dependence to self reliance; from distance to nearness to market places; from doubt to acceptance of modern technology; from theory to practice and from complacency to action. Keeping in view the SWOT analysis based on the experiences of the Expert Committee following recommendations were made at that time.

Status

The tea industry has reached a plateau absorbing development work and needs a paradigm shift to reach new heights of performance. Otherwise, the incremental yield progression will be minimal.

Potential

In the last decade, production of Kangra tea has increased from 6 to 14 lakh kg. The recommendations made here can lead to achievement of an ultimate potential detailed below:

(*a*) Rejuvenation: 2000 ha × 2500 kg = 50,000,00 kg
(*b*) Extension with in tea area: 1000 ha × 3000 kg = 3,000,000 kg
(*c*) New area: 2000 ha × 3000 kg = 6,000,000 kg
(*d*) Private Forest land: 5000 ha (not surveyed)
(*e*) Total estimated potential: 140 lakh kg +

Realization of this target will depend upon the implementation of the programme of development.

Single Window Approach

Multiplicity of agencies is leading to duplication and wasteful expenditure and contradictory advice. Coordination of these agencies is vital. Suggestions in this context are:

(*a*) Tea Board can act as the nodal agency for implementation of all development work.
(*b*) Inter departmental liaison between State agencies can be done by Tea Federation.
(*c*) Technical coordination for uniform agrotechnology can be the responsibility of Tea Board.

Land Policy

Changes are required for induction of professional investors and private entrepreneurs for opening up new areas as well as improvement of realization in traditional area through establishment of bought leaf factories. Facilities for long term leasing private plot and Government land could be provided to Tea Industry as has been done for the Tourism Industry.

Forest Policy

Rotational felling of excessive/unwanted shade trees within tea plantation is highly desirable. Tea is eco-friendly and provides an effective double canopy for soil and environmental conservation.

Manufacturing Capacity

(*a*) Optimization of existing manufacturing facilities for full capacity utilization.
(*b*) Combining the leaf of Bir tea factory with Baijnath tea factory, till adequate abandoned tea areas are regulated in Baijnath command area.

Planting Material

(*a*) The existing nurseries are from old local chinery bushes of low vigour which is known to perform very poorly. The plantation nurseries based on such material are not fit for extension planting and infilling.
(*b*) Improved planting materials comprising of clones and biclonal seed stocks found to be promising, should be officially released and used for future nurseries for distribution to the growers.

(*c*) Result demonstrations with improved quality of planting materials for extension and consolidation are essential.

Process Technology

Intensification of research on process technology for manufacture of high quality Kangra tea and incorporation of the findings in manufacturing process are recommended.

Incentives and Subsidies

We recommend phasing out of subsidies and implementation of incentive schemes.

Value Addition

A manual blending unit with a capacity of 1,000,00 kg should be established.

Extension Service

These are to be intensified:

(*a*) Demonstration particularly in non-traditional areas.
(*b*) Imparting training.
(*c*) Advisory visits.
(*d*) Literature.

Strengthening of Tea Board (Regional Office)

The Tea Board with lots of multifarious activities is under staffed. It should be strengthened with the additional technical staff to undertake surveys, monitor the implementation of various schemes and auditing the financial assistance.

6.2 Technical Officer (Tea)

The Government of Himachal Pradesh set up a separate cell to look after the dying tea industry of Himachal Pradesh, headed by the Technical Officer, Tea (TOT) at Palampur which has been placed under the

Department of Agriculture. Various inputs like chemical fertilizers, insecticides and pesticides, weedicides, implements and equipments, and planting materials were made available to the tea growers on subsidized rates. Prior to 1980 hardly any measures were taken for plant protection. Majority of tea planters are now protecting their gardens from diseases and pests by using recommended doses of pesticide and insecticides etc. Tea nursery of 2,00,000 plant capacity was maintained and efforts were initiated to bring more area under tea cultivation.

A brief account of the objectives and recent activities of the TOT wing are:

6.2.1 Objectives

(*i*) To rehabilitate the neglected and abandoned tea gardens.
(*ii*) To increase the production from the existing area.
(*iii*) To make the tea cultivation a profitable business.
(*iv*) To bring more area under tea.
(*v*) To introduce tea in non-traditional area of H.P.
(*vi*) To bring tea production per hectare at par with the other States having similar climatic conditions and variety.
(*vii*) To educate the tea planters and guide them to adopt the latest method of tea cultivation.
(*viii*) To improve the productivity quantitatively and qualitatively.

6.2.2 Activities

- A five year duration scheme to uplift the Schedule Caste Tea Planters of Himachal Pradesh was initiated during 2005-2006. 32,000 tea plants were distributed among them during the first year.
- An area of 130 kanal was brought under new plantation.
- Training camps to educate tea planters on various operations of tea cultivation were organized during 2005-2006.
- A scheme "Development of Tea Industry of Himachal Pradesh" has been submitted during 2005 to the Director of Agriculture for approval.

Various schemes being operated through the office of the TOT are presented in Table 6.4.

Table 6.4: Activities of Technical Officer (Tea)

1.	50% Subsidy on chemical fertilizer	(*a*) Ammonium sulphate (*b*) Single super phosphate (*c*) Muriate of potash
2.	50% Subsidy on Pesticides	(*a*) *Insecticides*: Endosulphan, Dichlorovos, Monocrotophos, Thimate, Achook (*b*) *Fungicides*: Hexaconzol, Copperoxichloride (*c*) *Herbicides*: Paraquate, Glyphosate, 2,4-D sodium salt
3.	50% Subsidy on tool & Equipment	(*a*) *Tool*: Pruning knife, Slashing knife, Hoe plain, Secateure, Pruning saw (*b*) *Equipment*: Spray pump, Power pump
4.	Identification of suitable area for tea cultivation in non-traditional area	Survey was conducted in Chamba, Mandi & Kangra districts and following areas were found suitable for tea cultivation: Chamba 1169 hectare, Mandi 2861 hectare, Kangra 1126 hectare
5.	Growing & distribution of improved tea plants to tea growers (Both seedling and clone)	Year — No. of Plants 1998-1999 — 1,50,390 1999-2000 — 1,43,585 2000-2001 — 1,62,850 2001-2002 — 1,48,350 2002-2003 — 72,305 2003-2004 — 51,290 2004-2005 — 42,345 2005 upto August — 1,52,550
6.	Extension programme	(*a*) Transfer of technology through personal visits of extension workers and organization of training camps. (*b*) Transfer of technology in the farmers fields through the demonstration plots. There are a total of 50 demonstration plots. 10 plots each of one acre area are taken each year for five years (*c*) Demonstration plots in non-traditional area: Areas identified in Chamba, Mandi and Kangra districts. Demonstration plots are set up to show the farmers of that area that tea can be cultivated in their area.

6.3 Miscellaneous

The Himachal Pradesh Horticultre Produce Marketing and Processing Corporation Ltd. (HPMC) has launched a blend of Kangra tea and the premium Himachal apple juice in tetra-packs in 2006.

The Trade-Related Aspects of Intellectual Property Rights (TRIPS) Agreement established certain obligations as regards to the protection of Geographical Indications (GIs). It is accordingly defined as "Indications which identify a good as originating in the territory of a member, or a region or locality in that territory, where a given quality, reputation or other characteristic of the good is essentially attributable to its geographical origin." The notions of "indications of source" and of "appellations of origin," which are used in the Paris Convention, encompass geographical indications as defined by the TRIPS Agreement.

Himachal Pradesh was among the first States in the country to formulate a policy for the registrations of Geographical Indications of products that originate in the State. Himachal Pradesh Patent Information Center (HPPIC) established by the Department of Science and Technology, Government of India had filed application on behalf of the manufacturers and Tea Planters' Association for the registration of Kangra Tea under Geographical Indications of Goods Act, 1999. The Registrar of Geographical Indications has issued a certificate in this regard from December, 2005. This will prevent unauthorized production using the Kangra Tea brand name on tea manufactured in areas other than Kangra; the place of its origin. As a consequence the Government of Himachal Pradesh is planning to organize workshops to formulate a marketing strategy for the stakeholders of Kangra Tea.

The cumulative efforts of years of Research and Development have shown positive results during the recent past but, the future seems to be more challenging.

7

Action Plan

The Strength-Weakness-Opportunity-Threat (SWOT) analysis on the tea of Himachal Pradesh points out to the following action plan:

SWOT

Strengths

- Pollution free environment.
- Less occurrence of diseases.
- Minimum use of synthetic insecticides and pesticides.
- Geographical Indications status.
- Health benefit grounds of tea.
- Well established research organizations.
- Numerous data available.

Weaknesses

- Low average productivity.
- Lack of promotional campaigning.
- Lack of internal market.
- Lack of information on economics and marketing aspects.
- No popular brand name.
- No value addition or product diversification.

Opportunities

- Changing consumers' preferences trends.

- State and Central tea promotion agencies are ready to invest in research and development.
- Geographical Indications status.
- Health benefits of tea drinking.

Threats

- Import of cheap tea.
- Opening of global market.
- Global warming.
- Increasing labour scarcity.

The traditional cup that cheers is being ceaselessly reinvented to come up to consumers' preferences which are changing. Billions of dollars are being spent in researching formulations and building brands world over. These are some of the challenges the Himachal tea industry is facing, due to which it is loosing its share in the market. Short-sightedness and ad hoc policy-making are further affecting the growth of tea industry in the state.

Following action plan is envisaged to boost the tea of Himachal Pradesh:

- Different agencies involved in research and development must have their mandates clearly defined to check duplication of work and wastage of resources.
- Cost of cultivation and producing tea needs to be brought down to encourage reinvestments.
- Application of modern techniques in tea cultivation and processing to cope up with the problems of labour shortage which is severely affecting the tea industry.
- Rejuvenation and repair of soil in the tea gardens need attention.
- New tea clones that would yield several times the current yield have to be established.
- Genetically engineered tea plants that have short dormancy period and are resistant to the changing weather conditions have to be developed.
- Plantation owners need to be made aware of the use of organic manure and biological control of pests.
- Distinct qualities of Kangra tea should be validated.

- Kangra tea must have its own brand name and logo.
- Visionary strategies for product innovation are needed to be framed.
- Opinion poll survey to explore the domestic market should be conducted.
- The Geographical Indications status of Kangra tea should be exploited in the national and international markets.
- Tea polyphenols that have been established to lend tea superior antioxidant property and health related benefits need to be studied in Kangra tea.
- For the satisfaction of quality conscious consumers, efforts to obtain ISO ratings for tea gardens and factories should be made.
- An aggressive promotional campaign using distinct qualities of Kangra tea should be undertaken.
- Communication means like internet should be used to promote marketing.
- Tea based product diversification should be encouraged.
- Human Resource Development through modern management skills.
- Mechanization and up gradation of tea factories.

Selected Bibliography

Annual Report of the Department of Commerce, Government of India, Chapter 8: Plantations and Agriculture.

Annual Reports, Institute of Himalayan Bioresource Technology, Palampur (H.P.): 1990-91; 1991-92; 1992-93; 1993-94; 1994-95; 1995-96; 199697; 1997-98; 1998-99; 1999-2000; 2000-2001; 2001-02; 2002-03; 2003-04; 2004-05.

Bhattacharya, A., Nagar, P.K. and Ahuja, P.S. 2002. Seed development in *Camellia sinensis* (L) O Kuntze. Seed Science Research 12: 39-46.

Bhattacharya, A., Nagar, P.K. and Ahuja, P.S. 2004. Change in endogenous indole-3-acetic acid and some biochemical parameters during seed development in *Camellia sinensis* (L) O Kuntze. Acta Physioligiae Plantarum 26(4): 399-404.

Dogra, R.K. and Paul, S. 2001. Genetic variability in local selections of tea [Camellia *sinensis* (L) O Kuntze] in Himachal Pradesh. *Himachal Journal of Agricultural Research* 27:71-76.

Dogra, R.K. and Paul, S. 2002. Association and path analysis studies in indigenous tea [*Camellia sinensis* (L) O. Kuntze] germplasm of HP. *In*: Proc. of the 15th Plantation Crops Symposium PLACROSYM-XV, Mysore, pp.154-60.

Empire Tea Centenary, 1938. 1986. *Tea Today*. Vol. 7, No. 4, 15-19.

Evaluation Report and Recommendations of Technical Expert Committee onIndustry of Himachal Pradesh. Conducted by Tea board, 14, B.T.M. Sarani, Calcutta-700001.

Gulati, A. and Ravindranath S.D. 1996. Seasonal variations in quality of Kangra tea [*Camellia sinensis* (L) O Kuntze] in Himachal Pradesh. *Journal of the Science of Food and Agriculture* 71: 231-36.

Gulati, A., Tamang, M.B. and Ravindranath, S.D. 1999. Clonal variations in quality related biochemicals in Kangra tea [*Camellia sinensis* (L) O Kuntze]. *Journal of Plantation Crops* 27 (3): 175-78.

Gulati, A., Gulati, A., Ravindranath, S.D. and Gupta, A.K. 1999. Variation in chemical composition and quality of tea (*Camellia sinensis*) with increasing blister blight (*Exobasidium vexans*) severity. *Mycology Research* 103(11): 1380-84.

Gulati, A., Ravindranath, S.D., Satyanarayana, G. and Chakrabarty, D.N. 1993. Effect of blister blight on infusion quality in orthodox tea. *Indian Phytopathology* 46: 155-59. 1994.

Gupta, S and Sharma, V., 1994. Kangra tea industry—problems and prospects. *The Assam Review and Tea News* (December): 20-24.

Gupta, S. and Sharma, V., 1995. Kangra tea industry—problems and prospects. *The Assam Review and Tea News* (January): 19-22.

Hackett, C.A., Wachira, F.N., Paul, S., Powell, W. and Waugh, R. 2000. Construction of a genetic linkage map for *Camellia sinensis* (tea). Heredity 85: 346-55.

http://tea.nic.in

http://www. teatalk. com

http://www.justtea.org

http://www.justtea.org/Links.htm

http://www.questia.com

http://www.teanorthwestindia.org/tea-industry-himachalteahistory.htm

http://wwwupasitearesearch.org

Kangra Tea by S.M. Dhar in *Tea Today*: (1992) Vol. 13 No. 2: 6-12. Published by Calcutta Tea Traders Association.

Kangra: The tea valley of Dhauladhar the white mountain range, Editorial in *Tea Today*: (1992) Vol. 13, No. 2: 6-12. Published by Calcutta Tea Traders Association.

Mann, A.S. 2003. *Economic analysis of marketing Kangra Tea: Emerging Problems and Prospects*. M.Sc. thesis. Department of Agriculture Economics,College of Agriculture, C.S.K.H.P.K.V., Palampur-176062 (H.P.), India. Sharma. p. 2003. Kangra tea cooperatives go through rough patch. *Hindustan Times*. June 1, 2003.

Mondal, T.K., Bhattacharya, A. and Ahuja, P.S. 2001. Induction of synchronous secondary somatic embryogenesis in *Camellia sinensis* (L) O Kuntze. *Journal of Plant Physiology* 158: 945-51.

Mondal, T.K., Bhattacharya, A., Sharma, M. and Ahuja, P.S. 2001a. Induction of i*n vivo* somatic embryos from tea (*Camellia sinensis*) colyldons. *Current Science* 81(3): 297-300.

Mondal, T.K., Bhattacharya, A., Sharma, M. and Ahuja, P.S. 2002. Factors affecting germination and conversion frequency of somatic embryos of tea [*Camellia sinensis* (L) O Kuntze]. *Journal of Plant Physiology* 159: 1317-21.

Mondal, T.K., Bhattacharya, A., Sharma, M. and Ahuja, P.S. 2002a. Propagation of tea [*Camellia sinensis* (L) O Kuntze] by shoot proliferation of alginate-encapsulated axillary buds stored at 4°C. *Current Science* 83(8): 941-44.

Mondal, T.K., Bhattacharya, A., Sood, A. and Ahuja P.S. 1998. Micropropagation of tea [*Camellia sinensis* (L) O Kuntze] using thidiazuron. *Plant Growth Regulation* 26: 57-61.

Mondal, T.K., Bhattacharya, A., Sood, A. and Ahuja, P.S. 2000. Factors affecting induction and cold storage of encapsulated tea [*Camellia sinensis* (L) O Kuntze] somatic embryos. *Tea* 21(2): 92-100.

Murashige, T. and Skoog, I. 1962. A revised medium for rapid growth and bioassay with tobacco tissue cultures. *Physiology Plant* 15: 473-97.

Pages from history. 1986. *Tea Today*. Vol. 7, No. 4: 21-29.

Paul, S. and Gupta,V.P. 1996. Adaptation of tea (*Camellia sinensis* (L.) O Kuntze) cultivars in Kangra Valley. *J. Plant Crops* 24 (Supp.) 487-89.

Paul, S., Gautam, R.K. and Sethi, G.S. 1996. Growth stimulating and retarding effects of gamma rays on two species of tea (*Camellia* sp) *J. Plant Crops* 24 (Supp.): 638-42.

Paul, S., Mishra, S.K. and Gupta, V.P. 1995. Evaluation, enhancement and conservation of tea germplasm in Kangra Valley. *Indian J. Pl. Genet.* Resources 8(2), 209-13.

Paul, S., Sharma, D.K., Sharma, K.L. and Mishra, S.K. 1994 Genetic variability for yield and quality in tea (*Camellia sinensis*) clones. *Indian Journal of Agricultural Science*. 64(5): 314-19.

Paul, S., Wachira, F.N., Powell, W. and Waugh, R. 1997. Diversity and genetic differentiation among populations of Indian and Kenyan tea (*Camellia sinensis* (L) O Kuntze) revealed by AFLP markers. *Theor Apple Genet* 94: 255-63.

Prakash, O., Sood, A., Sharma, M. and Ahuja, P.S. 1999. Grafting micropropagated tea [Camellia sinensis (L) O Kuntze] shoots on tea seedlings-a new approach to tea propagation. *Plant Cell Reports* 18: 883-88.

Saharan, G.S. and Chouhan, J.S. 1972. A survey of diseases of plants in Kangra district of Himachal Pradesh. *Journal of Research of Punjab Agricultural University* 9: 68-73.

Sandal, I., Bhattacharya, A. and Ahuja, P. S. 2001. An efficient liquid culture system for tea shoot proliferation. *Plant cell, Tissue and Organ Culture* 65: 75-80.

Sharma R. 1984. *An economic analysis of tea cooperatives (a case study of Bir Tea Cooperative factory of district Kangra*, Himachal Pradesh). M.Sc. Thesis. Department of Agriculture Economics, College of Agriculture, CSKHPKV, Palampur-176062 (H.P.), India.

Sharma, G., Sharma, K.L. and Sharma, C.M. 2001. Nutrient status of tea gardens of Himachal Pradesh-zone I. *Journal of Plantation Crops* 29(1): 44-48.

Sharma, M., Sood, A, Nagar, P.K., Prakash, O and Ahuja, P.S. 1999. Direct rooting and hardening of tea microshoots in the field. *Plant Cell, Tissue and Organ Culture* 58, 111-18.

Sharma, P., Pandey, S., Bhattachrya, A., Nagar, P. K. and Ahuja, P.S. 2003. Role of ABA and desiccation tolerance in somatic embryos of tea. *Indian Journal of Plant Physiology* (Special Issue): pp. 661-65.

Sharma, P., Pandey, S., Bhattachrya, A., Nagar, P.K. and Ahuja, P.S. 2004.

ABA associated biochemical changes during somatic embryo development in *Camellia sinensis* (L) O Kuntze. *Journal of Plant Physiology* 161: 1269-1276.

Sixty-eighth Report of the Department Related Parliamentary Standing Committee on Commerce under the chairmanship of Shri Murli Manohar Joshi on Action Taken by Government on the Recommendations of the Committee Contained in its Sixty-fourth Report on Export of Tea: Presented to the Rajya Sabha on the 14th March, 2005. Laid on the table of the Lok Sabha on the14th March, 2005.

Sixty-fourth Report of the Department-Related Parliamentary Standing Committee on Commerce on Export of Tea under the Chairmanship of Shri Kailash Joshi: Presented to the Rajya Sabha on the 19th August, 2003; Laid on the table of Lok Sabha on the 19th August, 2003.

Sood, A., Palni, L. M.S., Sharma, M., Rao, D.V., Chand, G. and Jain, N.K. 1993. Micropropagation of tea using cotyledon culture and encapsulatated somatic embryos. *Journal of Plantation Crops* 21 (supplement): 295-300.

Study to Promote the Industrial Exploitation of Green Tea Polyphenols in India. 2004. International Centre for Science and High Technology. United Nations Industrial Development Organization.

Sud R.G. and Badyal, J. 1989. Varietal and seasonal variations in chemical constituents of tea [Camellia sinensis (L) O Kuntze] in Himachal Pradesh. *Sri Lanka Journal of Tea Science* 58 (1): 73-78.

Sud, R.G. and Baru, A. 2000. Seasonal variations in theaflavins, thearubigins, total colour and brightness of kangra orthodox tea [Cemellia sinensis (L) O Kuntze] in Himachal Pradesh. *Journal of the Science of Food and Agriculture* 80: 1291-1299.

Sud, R.G. and Bhattacharjee, 1990. Quality evaluation of tea (*Camellia sinensis*) of Kangra valley. *Indian Journal of Agricultural Sciences* 60(10): 660-64.

Sud, R.G. and Bhattacharjee, 1992. Seasonal variations of theaflavins, thearubigins, brightness, colour, quality and mineral composition of kangra tea (*Camellia sinensis). Indian Journal of Agricultural Sciences* 62(2): 139-43.

Sud, R.G., Badyal, J., Bhan, S. and Misra, S.K. 1990. Estimation and seasonal variations of macro and micro nutrients in tea of Himachal Pradesh. *Sri Lanka Journal of Tea Science* 59(1): 29-36.

Sud, R.G., Prasad, R. and Bhargava, M. 1995. Effect of weather conditions on concentration of calcium, manganese, zinc, copper and iron in green tea [Camellia sinensis (L) O Kuntze] leaves of North-Western India. *Journal of the Science of Food and Agriculture* 67: 342-346.

Sud, R.G., Samkria, S., Gupta, M.K. and Kanwar, S.S. 2005. Fractionation of methanolic extract of tea [Camellia sinensis (L) O Kuntze] of Himachal Pradesh and evaluation for antibacterial activity. *Sri Lanka Journal of Tea Science*. (Accepted).

Sugha S.K. 1997. Perpetuation and seasonal build-up of *Exobasidium vexans*, causal agent of blister blight of tea in Himachal Pradesh. *Tropical* Science 37: 123-28.

Sugha S.K. and Singh, B.M. 1990. Comparative efficacy of fungicides against blister blight of tea (*EXOBASIDIUM VEXANS* MASSEE). *Indian Journal of Mycology and Plant Pathology* 20(3): 211-19.

Sugha, S.K., Singh B.M. and Sharma, K.L. 1990. Factors affecting development of blister blight of tea. *Indian Phytopathology* 43: 226.

Sugha, S.K., Singh, B.M., Sharma, D.K. and Sharma, K.L. (1991). Effect of blister blight on tea quality. *Journal of Plantation Crops* 19 (1): 58-60.

Sugha, S.K. and Paul, S. 1996. Effect of gamma-radiation on the development of blister blight. *J. Plant Crops* 24 (Suppl.): 243-45.

Tea Cultivation in Himachal Pradesh, 2000. Published by: Directorate of Extension Education, Himachal Pradesh Krishi Vishvavidyalaya, Palampur-176062 (H.P.), India.

Tea Directory of HP. Tea Board India. 1997. Published by Assistant Director, Tea Board, Palampur-176061 (H.P.), India.

Tea in the 21st century by Vijay Dudeja. A publication of Contemporary Tea Company Limited, 1 & 2 Old Court House Corner, Calcutta-700001.

Tea Research in HPKV Palampur. 2000. Published by: Department of Tea Husbandry and Technology, Himachal Pradesh Krishi Vishvavidyalaya, Palampur-176062 (H.P.), India.

Thakur, B.R. and Paul, S. 2002. Varietal tolerance/susceptibility of tea germplasm against blister blight. In: Proc. of the 15th Plantation Crops Symposium PLACROSYM-XV, Mysore, pp. 545-46.

The early History of Growth & Development of Tea Industry in Kangra District. By Sudripto Roy. In Kangra Tea Festival June 5-7, 1992, Palampur (H.P.).

The Heritage of Indian Tea by D.K. Taknet, Executive Publication, IIME, 1, Mahatma Gandhi Marg, Jhalana Institutional Area, Jaipur-302004 (India).

Index

Agrobacterium-mediated genetic transformation 90
agro-climatic conditions 31
Amplified Fragment Length Polymorphism 94
Antibactrial Activity 95
Application of modern techniques in tea cultivation 120

Ballard, R.A. 15
biochemical constituents, variations in 73
Blister Blight 80
Botanical North-West Provinces 21
Bruce, Robert 13
Bundla Tea Estate, Gold Medal Award 19

Calcutta Stock Exchange 15
Calendar of Tea Operations 43–44
Chambi tea estate 92
chemical fertilizers 116
Chinery type tea 34
cold storage, germination efficiency of 89
collateral host 81
Cooperative Marketing Society 113
Cooperative Tea Factories and Marketing Society 25
Cooperative Tea Factory 26
Council of Scientific and Industrial Research (CSIR) 23, 87
CSK Himachal Pradesh Krishi Vishvavidyalaya 5, 18, 30

Department of Tea Husbandry and Technology 31, 43, 73
Dhauladhar range 14, 29
Disease Management 57

Elite Planting Material 51
embryo abscisic acid 91
Entomology 51

Falconer, Dr. 14
farm yard manure 58
flavour reduction in tea 86
Forest Policy 114

Genetically engineered tea plants 120
Geographical Indications 28, 118, 121
Geographical Indications of Goods Act 118
Green and Black tea 25, 58

Hailey Nagar Tea Estate 14
Himachal Pradesh Horticultre Produce Marketing and Processing Corporation Ltd. 118
Himachal Pradesh Patent Information Center 118
Himalayan wild flora 58
Holta Tea Company 15

IHBT-Hill Area Tea Science 30
Indian Bankers' Association 105
Indian Tea Licensing Committe 18
Indo-German Dhauladhar Project 25
Infrastructural Constraints 113
insecticides and pesticides 31, 116
Institute of Himalayan Bioresource Technology (IHBT) 7, 23, 30, 51, 87
Intercropping in tea 102

ISO ratings for tea gardens 121

Tel Clones, New
  Kangra Asha 32
  Kangra Jwala 32
Kangra Tea Association 18
Kangra Tea Festival 26
Kangra Tea Planters 15, 18, 23
Kangra Tea 14–15, 22, 32
Kangra tea, characteristics of 99
Kangra tea, known for distinctiveness 5

Land Policy 114
Limited Liability Act 15
Lord Cavendish Bentinck 13–14

Manufacturing Capacity 114

Nagrota Bagwan 14
Nassan Tea Company 14
National Bank for Agriculture and Rural Development 25
National Tea Research Foundation 103
necrotic blisters 81
non-traditional tea area of Himachal Pradesh 54
North East and United Planters' Association 103
Nutrient management 102

Operational Constraints 110
organic farming 57, 99

Palampur Cooperative Tea Factory Limited 18, 26, 73
Pesticide Residue Studies 55
Policy Constraints 110
poor management of tea gardens 61
Price Stabilization Fund Scheme 107
Product Diversification 58
Propagating Techniques 32
Pruning operation 37

Ready-to-drink 58
Rejuvenation of Abandoned Tea Gardens 38, 55
repair of soil in the tea gardens 120

Schedule Caste Tea Planters, upliftment 116
Single Window Approach 113
Skiff operation 37
soil plant nutrient status 102
Special Tea Term Loan 105
Strength-Weakness-Opportunity-Threat (SWOT) analysis 119–10
Supply and Marketing Cooperative Industrial Society 23
Survey Report 24
synthetic chemicals, effects of 99

Tea Act 103
Tea Advisory Committee 106
Tea Board India 18, 24, 31, 103
  Functions of the 105
  responsibility of 114
Tea Breeding 92
Tea Diseases 80
Tea Experiment Station 73, 95
Tea Husbandry 51
Tea Plant Management 36
Tea Processing 51
  upgradation of a 109
Tea Research Association 52, 103
Tea Research Center 103
Technical Officer, Tea 25, 115
Tissue Culture 87
Trade Related Aspects of Intellectual Property Rights 28, 118

vermin-culture technology 102

weedicides 116
World Trade Organization 28, 101

Young Tea Plant Management 35, 51